YOUR CAR fault finder

Other titles in this series:

MOTORBIKE mechanics
What to FREEZE and how
YOGA for you
How to play TENNIS
PHOTOGRAPHY made easy

YOUR CAR fault finder

Text by John Day B.Sc(Eng), M.I. Mech.E.
Illustrations by R. Deynis
with Mike Twite
Series Editor P. Cassidy

Mirror Books

Published by Mirror Books Ltd.,
Athene House, 66/73 Shoe Lane,
London EC4P 4AB
for Mirror Group Newspapers Ltd.

Paperback edition June 1980

Produced for Mirror Books Ltd by
Chancerel Publishers Ltd.,
40 Tavistock Street,
London WC2E 7PB.

ISBN 0 85939 215 5

Origination by ReproSharp, London EC1.

Printed in Great Britain by
Richard Clay (The Chaucer Press) Ltd.,
Bungay, Suffolk, England.

CONTENTS

Chapter One

THE BASIC CAR

A motorcar is basically nothing more than a metal box resting on wheels. Some of the more familiar parts of the car are provided for the passengers' comfort and convenience. Others enable the driver to control it. And still others, usually out of sight, start, stop and power it. This list, of the principal parts of a car will enable you to identify key components, see how they work and eventually diagnose faults in them.

The essential parts of the engine

The way in which the parts of the car are distributed round the body varies. Most cars have a front engine, driving either the front or rear wheels. Some cars have a rear engine driving the rear wheels, while a few sports models have a mid-engine driving the rear wheels. The steering wheel is always connected to the front wheels, while brakes are fixed to all four wheels.

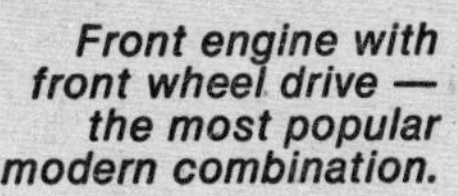

Front engine with front wheel drive — the most popular modern combination.

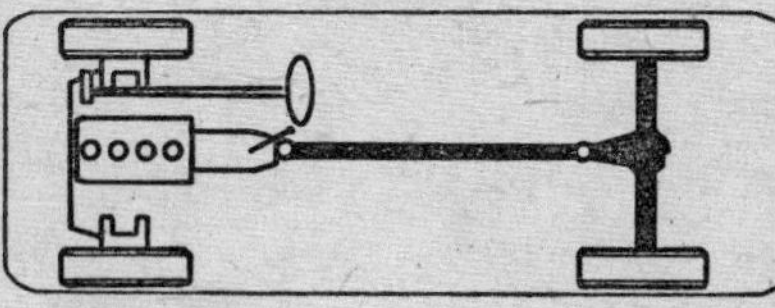

Front engine with rear wheel drive — simple and traditional.

Rear engine with rear wheel drive — becoming a less common design.

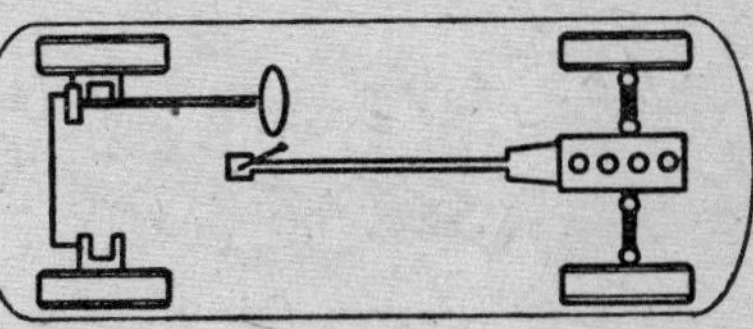

Wheels cannot work — steering, driving or breaking the car — unless they are in contact with the road. The road is always uneven, so the wheels are spring-mounted, by means of the suspension, to the corners of the box bottom, so that they remain in contact with the road surface.

As well as moving the car, the engine drives an electrical **generator** to provide electricity for the engine's **ignition system,** the lights and many other aids to driving, such as the windscreen wipers and the horn. Some modern cars even have micro-processors to monitor fuel consumption and provide the driver with information. In addition, the generator charges a **battery,** or accumulator, that provides current for an electric motor for starting and to allow the lights to be switched on when the engine is not running.

The **fuel** for the engine is petrol. It consists of hydrogen and carbon which, when mixed with oxygen from the atmosphere, burn very rapidly, turning into carbon dioxide and water. From the fuel tank the pertrol is pumped up to a device called a **carburettor** (derived from the word carbon) that mixes the fuel and air in the proper proportions for burning. This proportion is around 17 parts of air to one part of petrol by weight. Too much air, or oxygen, results in a weak mixture that is difficult to ignite and burns at too high a temperature for the good of the engine. Too little oxygen, and the burning is incomplete so that some of the petrol is wasted. The carburettor also breaks down the liquid into

Engine layout

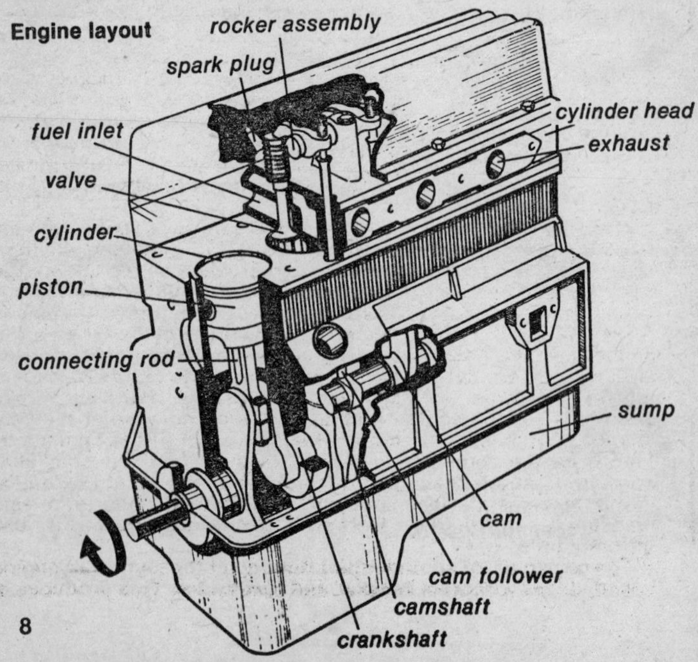

a fine mist so that it can mix easily with the air. This air/petrol mist is fed into a hole at the top of the engine called an inlet port.

The engine itself consists of a rectangular metal block with from two to eight (usually four to six) perfectly round and parallel holes in line in the block. These holes are the **cylinders.** Another piece of metal, the **cylinder head,** is bolted over the top to seal the cylinders.

In the cylinder head, round the top end of each cylinder, are three holes. Two of these holes are closed by mushroom shaped **valves** and the third is closed by a screwed **sparking plug.** Springs are fitted round the stems of the valves to hold them tightly closed except when the ends of the stems are pushed so that the valves open. One of these valves on each cylinder blocks off the inlet port from the carburettor and the other closes a second passage, or exhaust port, leading to the fresh air via the exhaust pipe. Two wires stick out of the cylinder end. One is fixed to the plug body and the other held in a central tube of insulating material. These wires, or plug points, have a small gap between them so that an electric spark can jump the gap to set light to the petrol/air mixture in the cylinder.

A hollow circular piece of aluminium, the **piston,** which is like an inverted jam pot, slides up and down inside each cylinder bore. A rod (the **gudgeon pin**) is fixed across the inner diameter of the piston. Another rod, the **connecting rod,** is pivotted onto the gudgeon pin. The other end of the connecting rod is pivotted to the handle part of a crank. Each cylinder has its own crank and all these cranks are formed on one piece of steel called a **crankshaft.** The crankshaft is carried in **bearings** in a box fitted under, or as part of, the cylinder block. The box has a bottom cover to keep the lubricating oil from leaking on to the road. This is the **sump.** When a piston is pushed down the connecting rod and the crank will change its straight line movement into a rotation of the crankshaft. The ends of the crankshaft stick out of the ends of the crankcase, so its rotation can be harnessed as driving power. Equally, if the crankshaft is rotated, the pistons will move up and down the cylinders.

One end of the crankshaft drives the car, through a **clutch** and **gearbox,** and the other shaft end carries a sprocket, driving a chain that goes round another sprocket twice as big. This larger sprocket is on a shaft that has a number of pear-shaped lumps, called **cams,** fixed to it. There are the same number of cams as there are valves in the cylinder head, two per cylinder, so a four cylinder engine has eight valves and eight cams. A set of levers are arranged so that the end of each one rests on the surface of one of the cams. As each cam rotates the lever will remain stationary as long as it is resting on the round base of the pear-shaped cam. It will only move when the point of the cam comes round. As the camshaft is being driven at half the crankshaft speed (due to the chain gearing) and the lumps do not extend all round the cams, the levers only lift for less than a quarter of each crankshaft's revolution. Moreover, levers can each lift at a different time.

The camshaft, or another shaft running at the same half engine-speed, drives a **contact breaker** and **distributor.** This produces an electric spark across the gap between the spark plug points exactly when it is needed, and then distributes the spark to each spark plug in turn.

How the parts work to provide power

Each piston goes through a cycle of four movements, starting with the piston at the top of the cylinder.

1. Induction

The crankshaft turns half a revolution and, in so doing, pulls the piston down the cylinder bore. As this is happening, the camshaft opens the inlet valve. Air rushes through the carburettor and picks up the air/petrol mixture, which fills up the space left by the descending piston.

2. Compression

By the time the piston begins to rise again, the cam lump has moved away from the rocker and the spring has shut the valve. The piston continues to rise and compress the mixture imprisoned in the cylinder. It is essential for the mixture to be compressed since it then gives the strongest possible burn when it is set alight.

3. Ignition

When the mixture is fully compressed, and the piston has returned to the top of its stroke, the spark jumps across the plug points to set fire to the mixture. The burning happens very quickly and the heat it produces makes the gases expand, producing the power to push the piston back down to the bottom end of its stroke, making the crankshaft rotate.

4. Exhaust

Finally, the piston rises up the cylinder again and a cam opens the exhaust valve. Thus the burnt gas can be pushed out through the exhaust port to the exhaust system. Then when the piston reaches the top of the cylinder, the whole cycle begins again.

Since the piston is only moved by the pressure of the burning gas for one of its four strokes, something else must move the piston through the other three. Two things do this. Firstly, a heavy **flywheel** on the outer end of the crankshaft keeps things going and, secondly, the other cylinders have their power strokes at different times as the crankshaft goes round.

When the fuel burns in the cylinders it not only heats the gas to push the pistons down, but heats the engine itself. If the engine heating was allowed to continue, some of the parts would get red hot and some even melt. So the cylinder block and the cylinder head are made hollow, so that cooling water can circulate round them. The water is pumped via a **radiator** that cools it and this keeps the engine at a safe and efficient working temperature.

Adjustments for efficient running

One of the effects of engine heat is that the stems of the valves expand as they get hot. Obviously the valve heads must seal against the ends of the inlet and exhaust ports at all times so an adjusting screw is incorporated in one end of the rocker. This **tappet screw** allows the cam, rocker and valve stem system to be set up with just enough clearance to allow the valve to shut when it is hot. Tappet clearances need to be adjusted to compensate for both expansion with heat and with wear. If the tappet clearance is too small the valve will not shut properly, the gas will not be compressed as much as it should be and some of the power gas pressure will be lost. If the clearance is too great the valves will not open long enough for sufficient gas to get through.

To get the spark at the right time in the engine cycle it is essential that the **contact breaker** and **distributor assembly** are properly adjusted. When the petrol mist is set alight it does not all burn instantaneously. Instead it burns outwards from the sparking plug. This takes a little time in relation to what is happening to the moving parts. To get the greatest pressure on the piston for the longest part of its stroke and, therefore, let the fuel do the most good, it is necessary for the spark to jump the plug gap just before the piston has reached the top of its compression stroke. This advance of the spark gets the mixture burning well and pressure building up just as the piston goes over the top and down on the power stroke.

If the spark takes place too soon (too much in advance) the pressure will build while the piston is still moving upwards so that power is lost and the engine makes a tinkling noise, called 'pinking'. This is not good for it. A similar state of affairs can be produced by using too low a grade of fuel, which can be ignited by the heat produced by compression. It also happens if the engine is running too slowly under a heavy load caused by, for example going up a steep hill in too high a gear, or using the wrong sparking plugs, in which case the points get red hot and set light to the mixture before the spark is produced.

Power from the engine to the wheels

The internal combustion engine has two disadvantages as an engine for a motorcar. Firstly, it cannot be started and stopped in the same way a car is started and stopped, and secondly it has to be running fairly fast before it will provide any appreciable amount of power.

To allow the engine to run when the car is stopped a device known as a **clutch** is provided. The back face of the flywheel is smooth and a disc covered with friction material is pressed against the smooth surface by a spring. The disc is connected to a shaft connected to the gearbox. A lever mechanism is arranged so that, when the clutch pedal is depressed, the load of the spring can be taken from the disc. When full spring strength clamps the disc to the flywheel the gearbox shaft is driven. But when the spring is released, by depressing the clutch pedal, the flywheel can turn without dragging the disc round and the drive to the gearbox ceases.

To overcome the second snag the car has gears. The problem is that at 1,000 revolutions per minute (rpm) the engine produces a negligible amount of power. It produces a maximum power at around 5,000 or 6,000 rpm whereas the road wheels have to be turned at something between zero rpm (at a standstill) and around 1,000 rpm (at full speed). Further, higher power is wanted to get up hills and to accelerate the weight of the car, so it is essential to have gears that will allow the engine to work at the rpm needed for the power requirements, while turning the wheels at no more than the desired road speed. This is achieved by means of a box containing several sets of gear ratios that can be selected according to the needs of car and engine. Moreover, as the engine will not run backwards, an extra set of gears to give reverse is included. The gearbox is connected to the wheels by an **output shaft** and a **final drive** unit.

The final drive has two jobs to do. Firstly to give an overall speed reduction of between four and five to 1 so that the road wheels run at a quarter to a fifth of the speed of the gearbox output shaft. Secondly, to provide a drive to both wheels even though they are turning at different speeds when the car goes round a bend and the outer wheels have to travel further than the inside wheels in the same amount of time. This compensation for cornering wheel speeds is done by a fascinating but complex set of gears known as a **differential.**

Steering the car

The fact that the inside and outside wheels of a car going round a bend have to move round curves of a different radius also affects steering. For a car to go round a bend without any of the tyres being scrubbed sideways, the **axles** of all four wheels, must point to centre of the bend. The two back wheels are on one axle and thus the bend centre must be on a line that is a continuation of this axle. The two front wheel axles must also point towards this same bend centre, but not being on the same axle, they must turn through slightly different angles.

To get this effect the two **steering arm levers** connected to the front wheel axles are angled slightly inwards. They are set so that two imaginary lines drawn through the pivot (about which the wheels swivel) and the ends of the levers would meet in the middle of the back axle when the wheels are straight ahead. The ends of

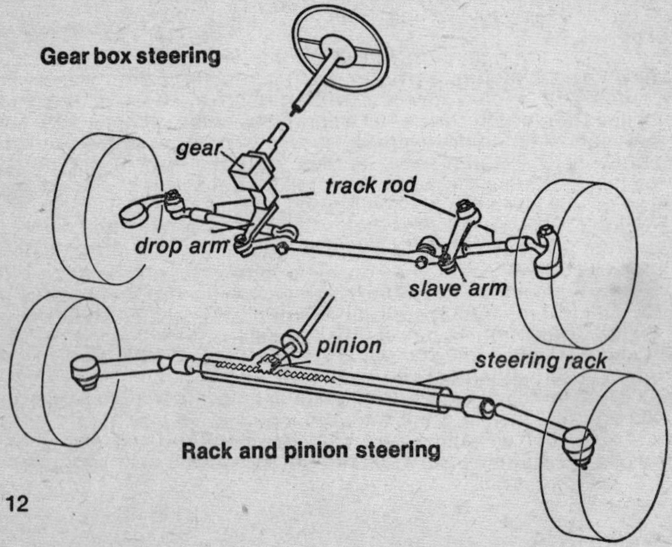

the steering arms are connected together with a rod having a swivel joint at each end, the **track rod.** This rod is moved sideways by gearing at the bottom end of the steering column, which is connected to the driver's steering wheel.

To get the car to steer straight ahead automatically when the driver leaves go of the steering wheel, the front wheels are provided with **castor action.** Were this not so, cars would be very tiring to steer and tend to weave all over the road. This castor action is similar to that of castors on furniture in that the point where the wheel meets the road is behind the axis about which the wheels swivel.

Suspension for comfort and safety

If the wheels, and so the tyres, are to be kept in constant contact with the road, so that they can drive and steer properly, they must be sprung from the body box. Often the rear axle supports the body through long curved **leaf springs** clamped to the body floor at their ends and to the axle at their centres. These do the double duty of springing the axle and at the same time locating it in its proper place.

The front wheels are independently sprung so that the movement of one, on a bump, does not affect the other wheel. It is important that the wheels should stay as near as possible at right angles to the road for the **tyre treads** to grip correctly. Also the wheels must stay the same distance apart to prevent the tyres scrubbing sideways and wearing out.

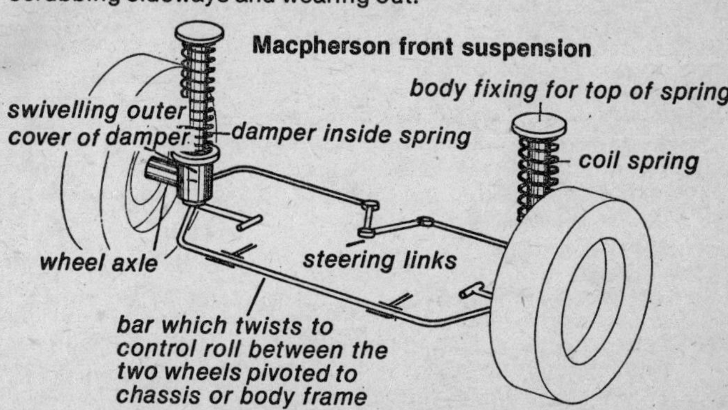

To try and get as near as possible to these ideal conditions the steering pivots are hinged top and bottom to the body box by A-shaped levers. The tops of the As are pivoted to the wheel swivel pin and the bottoms of the As to the body. A coilspring acts between the bottom of the A and body box and a **shock absorber** is mounted inside the spring.

The shock absorber is there to dampen the movement of the spring. Every spring has a frequency at which it will vibrate and, if a car spring was undamped, it would tend to bounce the wheels off the road.

Chapter 2

TOOLS FOR THE JOB

Keeping a car safe and in good running order throughout its long-distance life needs know-now, time and good tools. Know-how is contained in these pages. Time you will need, both to spend on the essential work and to think about the job and not botch it by hurrying. Tools will have to be bought.

Invest in the best

When buying tools it is extravagant to buy cheap, poor tools for they will never do a good job and they will not last all that long. Good tools are expensive and need looking after. Treat them with respect and only use them for the jobs they were designed to do.

To use a tool wrongly can at times be dangerous. A badly fitting spanner can slip and cause bruised knuckes or a gashed hand. Using a file as a lever can result in it shattering like glass and flying into your face.

The tools you buy should only be the ones you need. The big expensive sets look impressive, but think first. Will you ever need all of them? For instance, there are sets with spanners for British, American and metric size nuts, but your car will only use one kind so why waste money on the other two? Some jobs need special tools that will only do that one job on one make, or model, of car. These can often be hired for the single occasion more cheaply than they can be bought.

Special tools and jury rigs

Often a special tool can be made up, or something can be rigged up to serve. To remove an oil filter canister usually calls for a special wrench to grip the smooth round surface. But a filter can just as easily be turned using a length of webbing strap with the ends clamped together with a Mole wrench. An oversize open jaw spanner can be temporarily brought down in size by putting a piece of metal, or a coin, between one jaw and the flat of the nut — but put the packing under the jaw that is pushing and not the other which is pulling.

Important safety rules

For your own protection there are several safety rules which you must remember when working on a car.

1. Remove the ignition key so that the engine will not start by accident. It is better still, or essential if you are working on the electrical system, to remove the earth lead from the battery. This is the thick braided cable bolted at its other end to the car body.

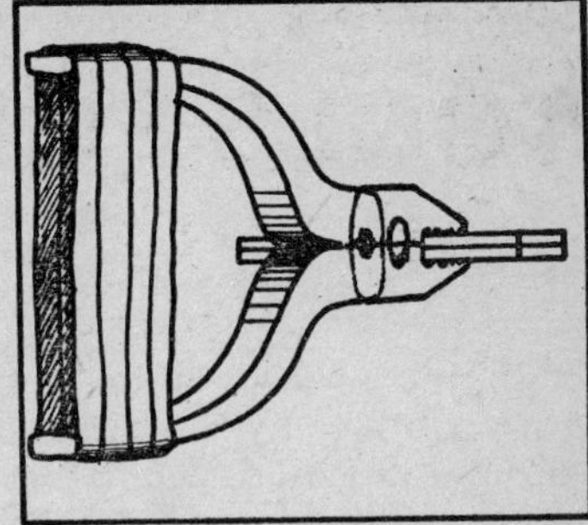

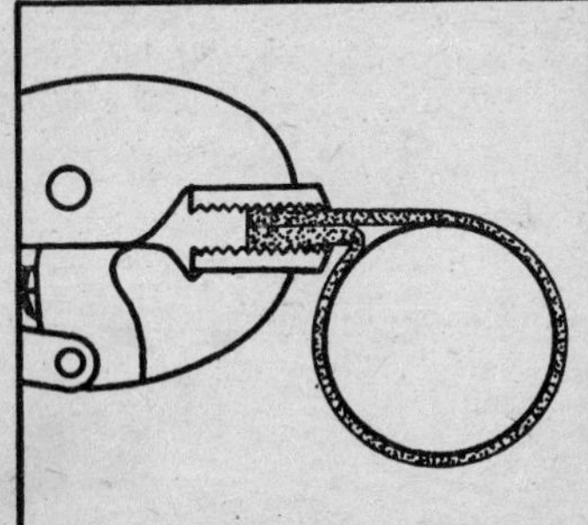

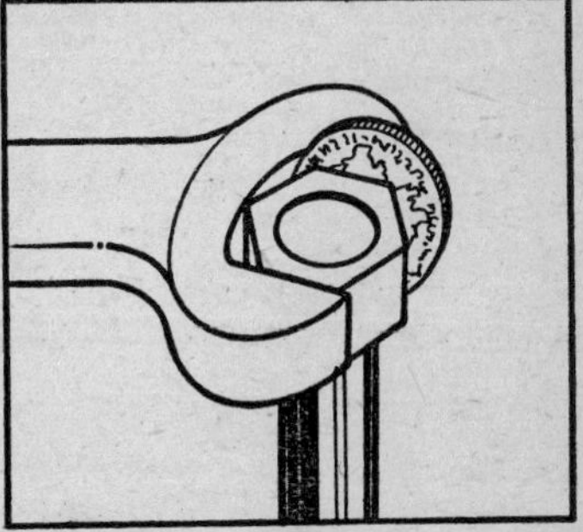

Top left: two pieces of wood with twisted ropes at each end will compress a spring.

Top right: pliers with a rubber band on the handles will make a temporary clamp.

Lower left: grip large round objects like oil filters with a strap and Mole wrench.

Lower right: use a coin to make an oversize spanner fit a smaller nut.

2. Don't smoke when you lean over a battery. The battery gives off hydrogen and oxygen, which can explode and blow the battery apart spraying everything with corrosive sulphuric acid.

3. Be extra cautious if the engine is running and the bonnet open. Keep your hands well away from the pulleys, belts and the fan and above all never wear a loose tie, a pendant or anything else loose and dangling. These, or long hair, can be caught in a pulley and snatch your face down on to the moving machinery.

4. Never rely on the jack supplied if you are going to do any work on the car. The standard jack is too flimsy to stand anything except a straight lift. Always support the car on either proper rigid stands or blocks of wood. **Do not use bricks or lumps of concrete or stone,** as these will crack under the load and drop the weight of the car on anybody underneath.

5. Remember, when you are working on a car there may well not be anybody within calling distance to rescue you.

Minimum tool kit

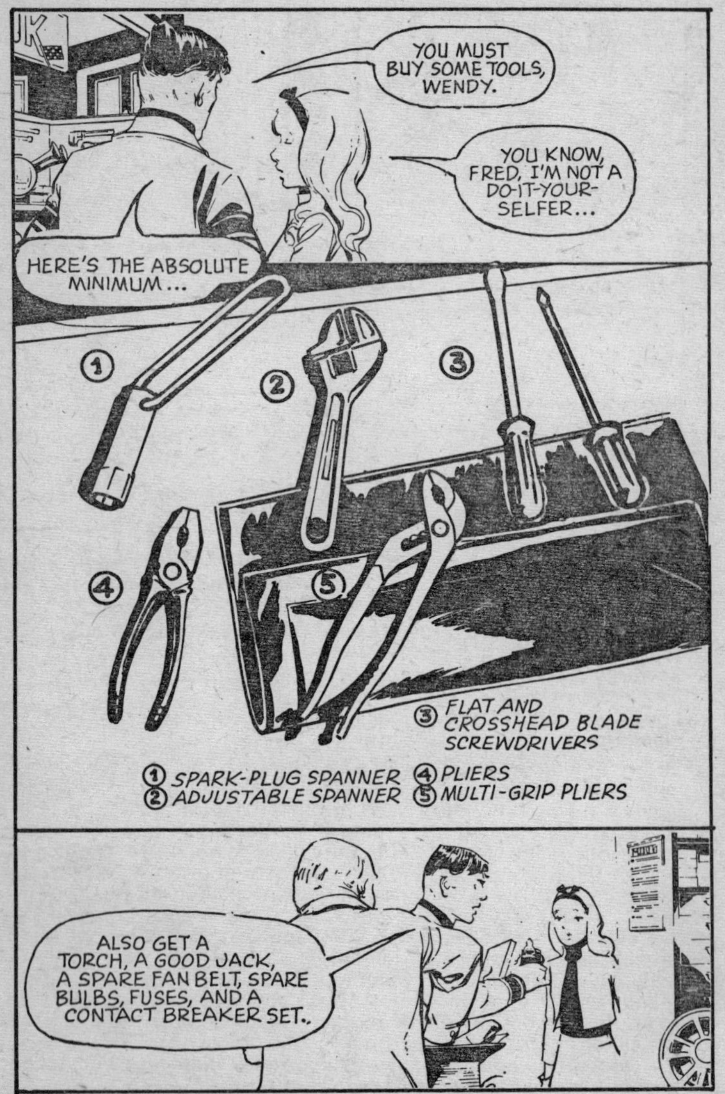

A good set of tools

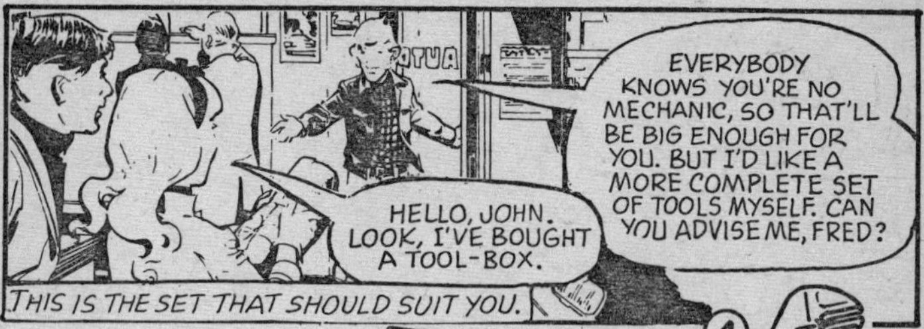

EVERYBODY KNOWS YOU'RE NO MECHANIC, SO THAT'LL BE BIG ENOUGH FOR YOU. BUT I'D LIKE A MORE COMPLETE SET OF TOOLS MYSELF. CAN YOU ADVISE ME, FRED?

HELLO, JOHN. LOOK, I'VE BOUGHT A TOOL-BOX.

THIS IS THE SET THAT SHOULD SUIT YOU.

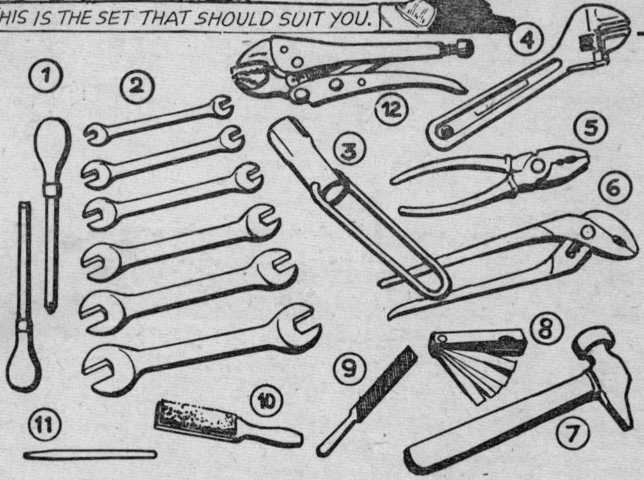

1. TWO TYPES OF SCREWDRIVER (FLAT AND CROSS-HEAD BLADES). 2. SET OF FLAT SPANNERS (8 TO 19 mm) (OR 7/16th IN TO 3/4 in AF). 3. SPARK-PLUG SPANNER. 4. ADJUSTABLE SPANNER 5. PLIERS. 6. MULTI-GRIP PLIERS. 7. HAMMER. 8. FEELER GAUGES 9. SMALL FILE FOR CLEANING POINTS. 10. WIRE BRUSH. 11. PUNCH 12. MOLE GRIP.

A first class tool set

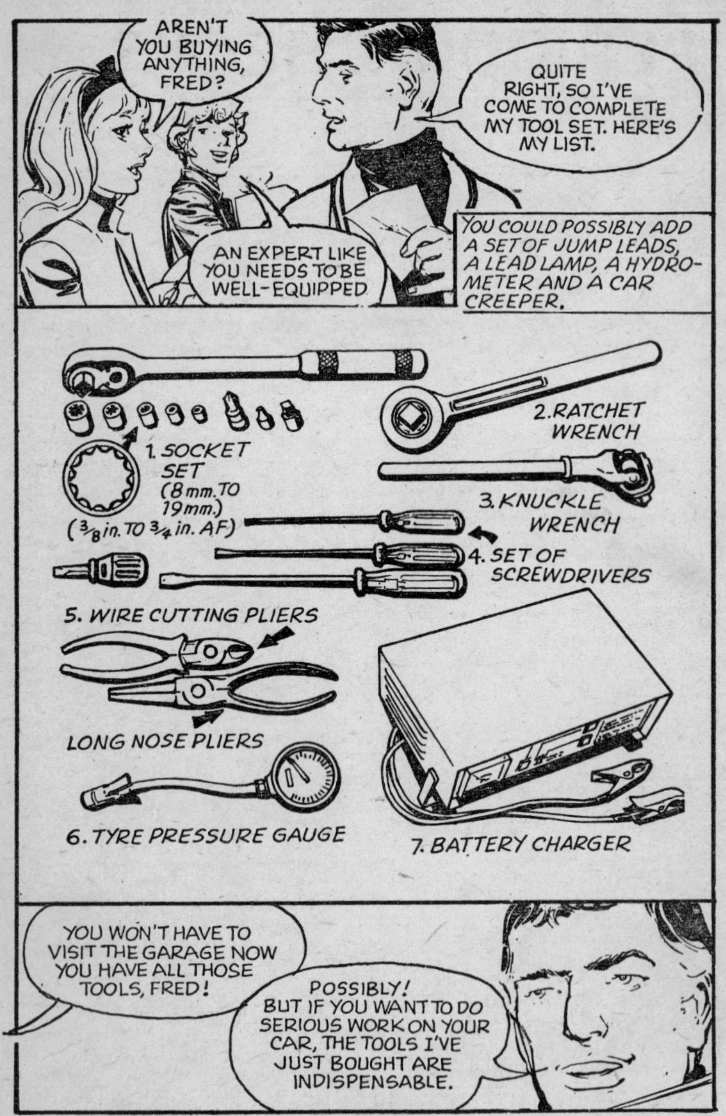

Chapter 3

PERIODIC CHECKS

Like most other things cars wear out. They use up their various fluids and their components get out of adjustment. To keep your car in a safe-to-drive condition and to help it to last as long as possible it is necessary to check certain things at various times. Keeping a car in good tune also means it will use less fuel and be easier to drive. This table gives an idea of what needs looking at and how frequently.

Check	Weekly or 250 miles	Monthly or 1,000 miles	6 Month or 5,000 miles
Engine oil level	X		
Tyre pressures	X		
Coolant level	X		
Battery level		X	
Brake fluid level		X	
Brake pad thickness		X	
Fan belt tension		X	
Valve clearances			X
Contact breaker point gap		X	
Clutch fluid level		X	
Windscreen washer bottle	X		
Gearbox oil level			X
Clean battery terminals			X
Drum brake lining thickness			X
Tyre tread depth			X

Cleaning the bodywork

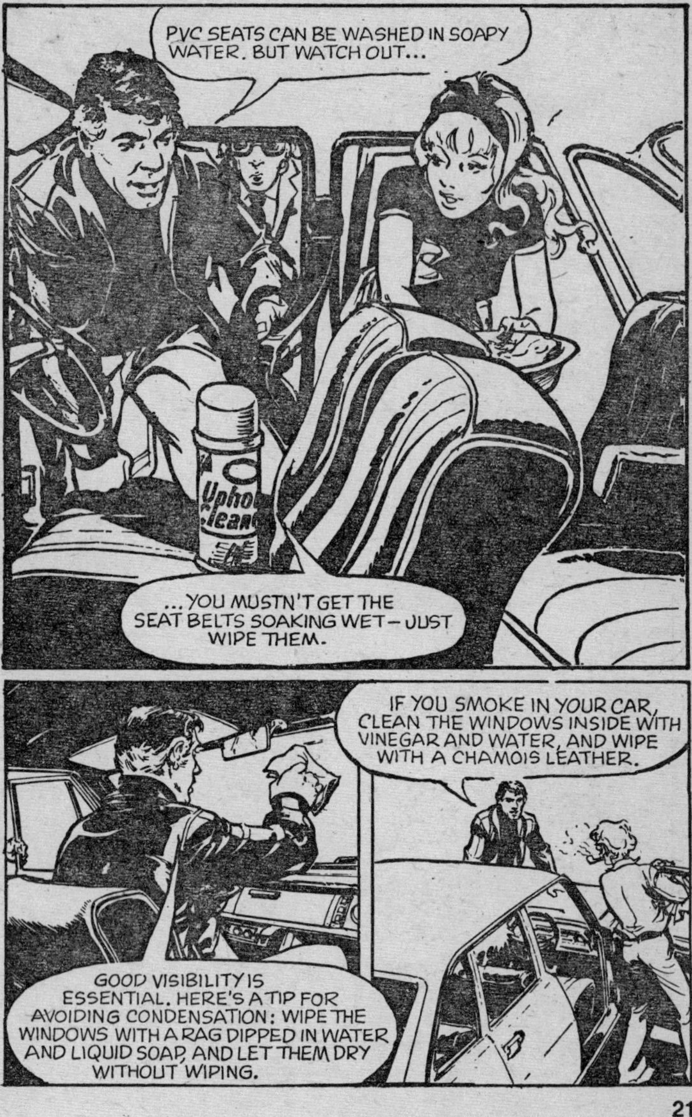

Cleaning the interior

PVC SEATS CAN BE WASHED IN SOAPY WATER. BUT WATCH OUT...

...YOU MUSTN'T GET THE SEAT BELTS SOAKING WET—JUST WIPE THEM.

I THINK I'M OUT OF OIL!
DIPSTICK
MIN
MAX
THE SPACE BETWEEN THE 'MAX' AND 'MIN' MARKS REPRESENTS ABOUT 30% OF THE TOTAL OIL CAPACITY. USUALLY A PINT WILL BRING IT BACK TO THE 'MAX' MARK.
TO MAKE SURE, PARK THE CAR ON A LEVEL ROAD AND WAIT ONE MINUTE FOR THE ENGINE OIL TO DRAIN DOWN TO THE SUMP. WIPE THE DIPSTICK BEFORE DIPPING IT INTO THE SUMP.
WATCH OUT IN SERVICE STATIONS.
MAKE SURE THE ATTENDANT HAS PUSHED THE DIP-STICK RIGHT IN.
FOR THE GEARBOX AND REAR AXLE, UNSCREW THE FILLER PLUGS. IF OIL DOESN'T RUN OUT, TOP UP SLOWLY UNTIL IT DOES. CHECK THE HAND-BOOK FOR THE CORRECT OILS.

Water levels and windscreen washers

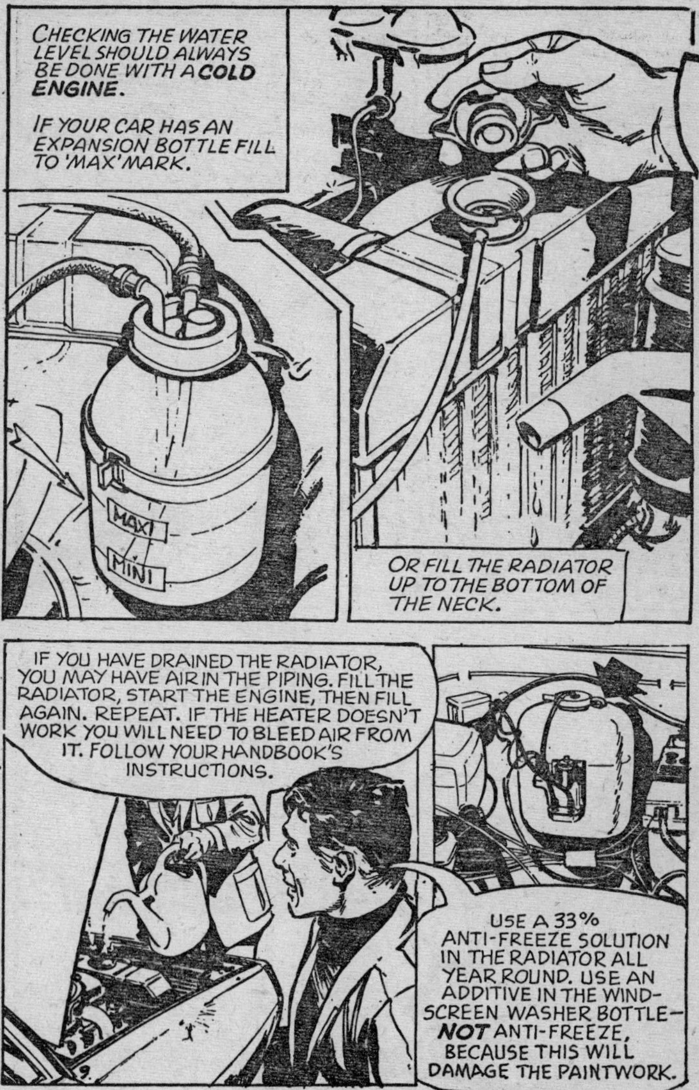

CHECKING THE WATER LEVEL SHOULD ALWAYS BE DONE WITH A **COLD ENGINE**.

IF YOUR CAR HAS AN EXPANSION BOTTLE FILL TO 'MAX' MARK.

MAXI

MINI

OR FILL THE RADIATOR UP TO THE BOTTOM OF THE NECK.

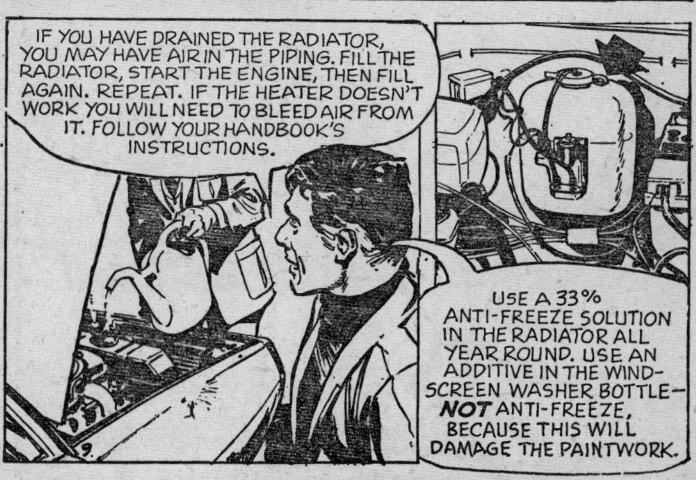

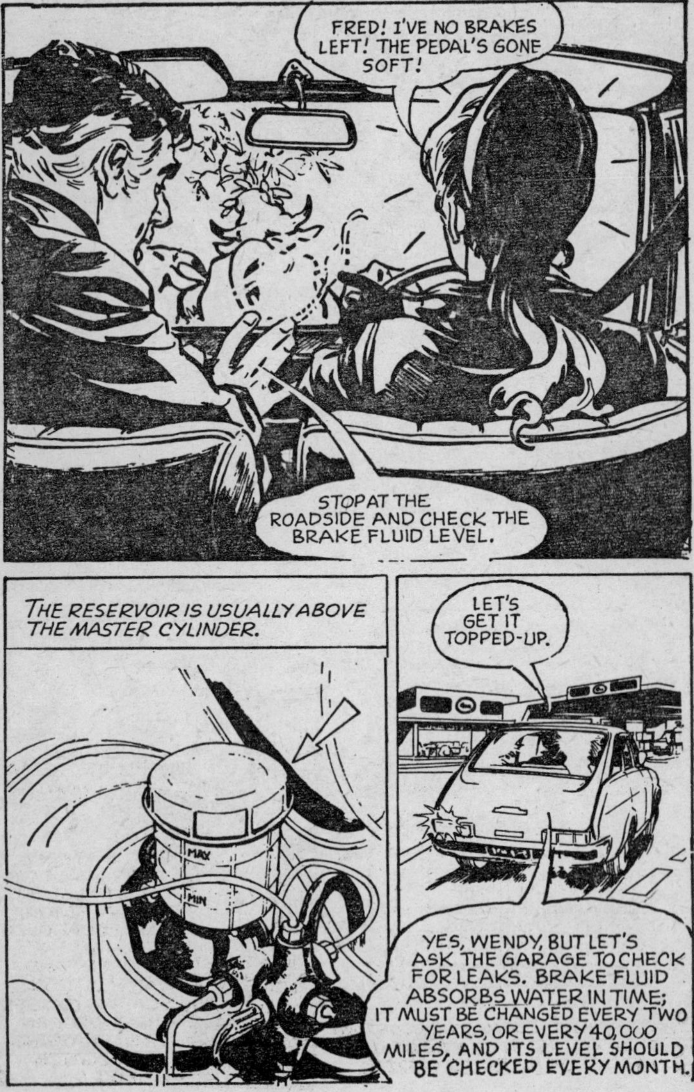

FRED! I'VE NO BRAKES LEFT! THE PEDAL'S GONE SOFT!

STOP AT THE ROADSIDE AND CHECK THE BRAKE FLUID LEVEL.

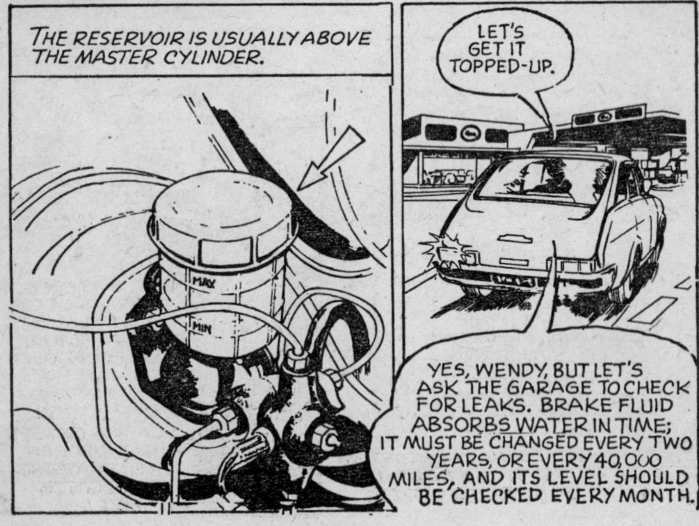

THIS WHITE DEPOSIT ON THE BATTERY IS ODD!

YES, IT'S SULPHATE. WHEN IT APPEARS YOU MUST CLEAN THE TERMINALS AND CLAMPS THEN COVER THEM WITH PETROLEUM JELLY.

THE CORRECT LEVEL OF ELECTROLYTE IS ABOUT ¼ IN. ABOVE THE PLATES YOU SEE WHEN YOU REMOVE THE STOPPERS. IF THERE ISN'T ENOUGH, ADD DISTILLED WATER.

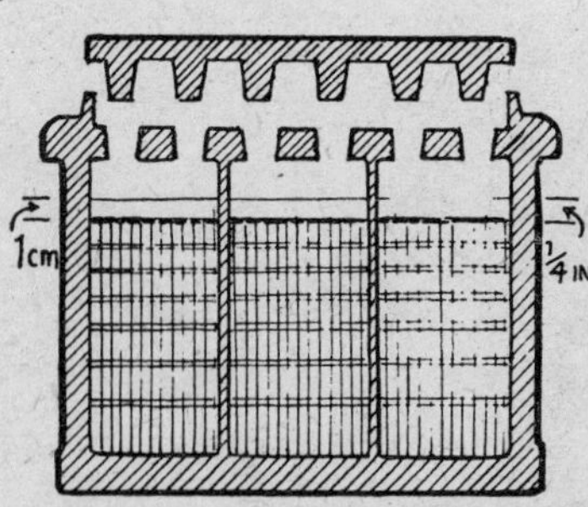

SAVE THE WATER WHEN DEFROSTING YOUR 'FRIDGE. IT CAN BE USED INSTEAD OF DISTILLED WATER.

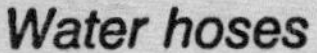

Water hoses

LOOK, THERE'S A BULGE ON THAT WATER HOSE!

YES, AND IT'S SERIOUS, BECAUSE A BURST HOSE CAN RESULT IN DAMAGE TO THE ENGINE.

AS SOON AS YOU SEE SIGNS OF WEAR (CUTS BESIDE THE FASTENING CLAMPS, CRACKING, BULGES, ETC.) CHANGE THE HOSE.

IS THAT DIFFICULT?

QUITE SIMPLE, AS LONG AS YOU USE THE CORRECT SIZE HOSE AND THE PROPER JUBILEE CLIPS. RUB A LITTLE SOAP INSIDE THE NEW HOSE IF IT WON'T PUSH ON.

Checking the wipers

Protecting rubber seals and door locks

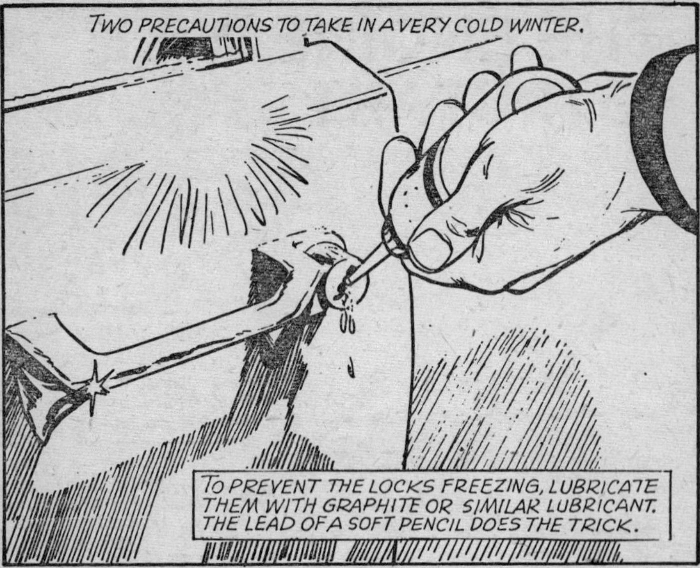

TWO PRECAUTIONS TO TAKE IN A VERY COLD WINTER.

TO PREVENT THE LOCKS FREEZING, LUBRICATE THEM WITH GRAPHITE OR SIMILAR LUBRICANT. THE LEAD OF A SOFT PENCIL DOES THE TRICK.

Chapter 4

THE ENGINE WILL NOT START

When the engine does not start it is usually, but not always, due to a fault in the electricals, either in the ignition or the starter circuits. While it is easy to check out most of the circuits, it helps a lot to know what is happening in the system.

For starting the car has a **battery,** or **accumulator.** It stores current for an electric **starter motor,** which rotates the engine, and for the **ignition system,** which provides the spark at the **sparking plug** gap. When the engine is running the battery is charged by an engine-driven **generator** and to show this is happening the red ignition light on the dashboard goes out. When the light is showing the battery is not being charged and the engine will only run as long as the battery charge lasts. If the headlights, or any other electrical devices, are switched on at the same time, the battery will discharge faster still.

How to produce 20,000 volts

The heart of the ignition system is the **ignition coil,** which consists of an iron core wound round with two coils of wire. One coil has relatively few turns of thick wire (the primary winding) and the other a large number of turns of thin wire (the secondary winding). When a voltage is applied across the ends of the primary winding, the iron core becomes magnetized. This rise in the magnetic field also goes through the secondary winding. When the current is switched off the sudden fall in magnetism produces a voltage in the secondary winding. Because secondary winding has many more turns than the primary, the secondary voltage is higher in proportion to the relative number of turns. In fact, with 12 volts across the primary, some 15,000 to 20,000 volts appear across the ends of the secondary winding — enough to give you an unpleasant shock. This is known as the **high tension (HT)** current and is sufficient to jump a spark across the 0.020in. gap of the sparking plug under the pressure of compression in the cylinder. This high voltage needs a lot of insulation, hence the thick rubber or plastic, covering of the HT cables.

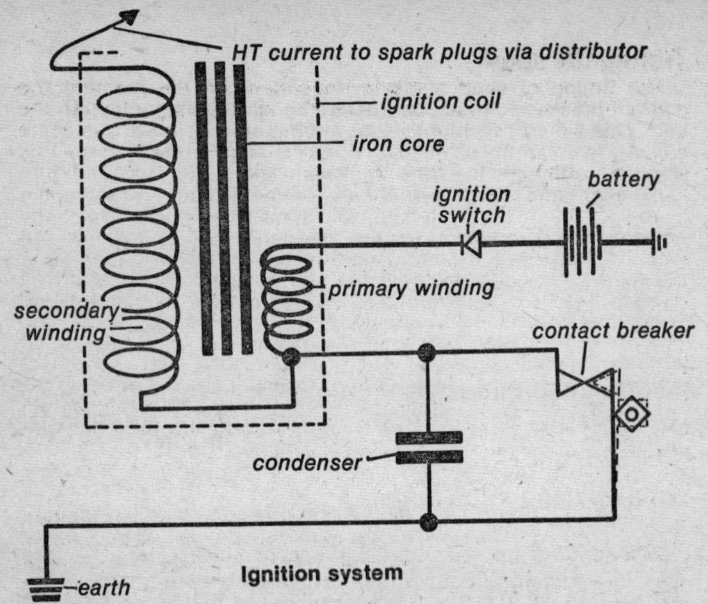

Ignition system

The switch for the primary winding is the **contact breaker.** This is a pivoted lever rocked against a spring by a cam driven at half crankshaft speed and carrying one contact point. The other contact point is adjustably fixed to a plate in the top of the contact breaker housing. The cam has the same number of humps as the engine has cylinders and, as it is driven at half speed, the lever is moved in synchronism with the need for one spark in each cylinder. When the points are closed, current flows from the battery, through the ignition switch to one side of the coil primary winding. The other side of that winding is connected to the contact breaker lever, which is insulated, then through the points to earth.

Distributing the HT current

This current builds up the magnetism in the coil core until it reaches a maximum strength. As soon as the cam hump, or lobe, meets the lever, the points open and the current suddenly ceases to flow, thus equally suddenly breaking down the magnetic field. This rapid reduction in magnetism produces an HT current in the secondary winding of the coil. This HT current from the coil is fed back to the insulated top cover of the contact breaker, the part that actually does the distributing. This distributor is an insulated arm fixed to the contact breaker cam and carrying a brass strip. The strip rotates with the cam and points in turn to contacts connected to each individual sparking plug. Thus each time an HT sparking voltage is produced by the contact breaker and coil system, the distributor decides which sparking plug needs the HT current to set light to the charge.

Timing the spark

The timing of each spark is dependent on the moment the contact breaker points separate and so kill the magnetism in the coil. This would be alright if the engine always ran at the same speed and under the same load. But a car engine does not run this way and, although the time the spark takes to get the mixture really alight and pressing on the piston stays much the same, the speed at which the piston moves does not. Neither does the pressure of compression remain the same — it depends on the amount of mixture passed by the throttle. To adjust the timing of the spark to the right moment the contact breaker cam is driven through a centrifugal weight system that moves the cam forward in relation to the speed increase in its driving shaft. To get the spark at the right time according to the amount of mixture going into the engine, use is made of the vacuum in the inlet ports to act on a diaphragm that is coupled to the contact breaker housing. As the vacuum increases due to a small throttle opening, the contact breaker is moved in relation to the cam and the time of point opening and thus the spark timing is adjusted to suit.

The essential condenser

There is one other very important component of the ignition system and that is a small metal cylinder, with one wire coming from its end, called the **condenser.** This has the ability to receive and store a rising voltage current and then to send it back in the opposite direction. When the contact breaker points open there is a tendency for even the low voltage to jump across the small gap as they begin to move. This sparking across the points would soon burn the metal surfaces and spoil the contact areas if it were not for the condenser that is connected across the points. Actually the outer metal body is clamped to earth in the contact breaker casing and the wire is connected to the insulated lead from the coil primary binding. Instead of jumping the breaker gap the current flows into the condenser and when the condenser is fully charged it bounces that current back into the primary winding in the opposite direction to help the very fast breakdown of the magnetism needed to produce enough volts for a good, fat spark.

Starting the engine

The **starter,** which also works off the battery, is an electric motor with a small gear carried on a very coarse screw thread on its shaft. As the starter motor begins to spin, the inertia of the gear, or pinion, tends to prevent it turning and the pinion screws itself along the starter shaft to engage its teeth with gear teeth cut in the rim of the engine flywheel. As soon as the engine starts, the flywheel drives the pinion faster than the starter motor, and the pinion is screwed back along the shaft so the teeth are out of engagement.

Since it takes a fair amount of power to turn a cold engine fast enough to get it started, and the electrical system is only 12 volts, a very heavy current is needed and hence the starter cables are very thick.

Engine won't start — check the battery

Engine won't start — check the wiring

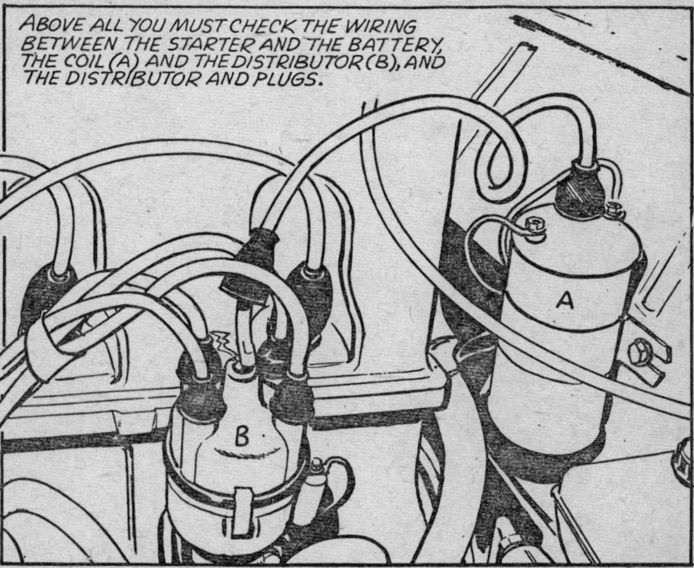

ABOVE ALL YOU MUST CHECK THE WIRING BETWEEN THE STARTER AND THE BATTERY, THE COIL (A) AND THE DISTRIBUTOR (B), AND THE DISTRIBUTOR AND PLUGS.

A

B

YOU LOOK IN A MESS! COME ON, WE'LL LOOK AT THIS TOGETHER.
IT WON'T START. AND I CAN'T FIND ANYTHING WRONG. IT'S ENOUGH TO DRIVE YOU MAD!
IF YOUR ENGINE WON'T TURN WHEN THE BATTERY IS FULLY CHARGED AND THE CONNECTIONS ARE GOOD, IT COULD BE STARTER FAILURE OR A JAMMED STARTER.
HOW DO I FREE IT IF THE STARTER'S JAMMED?
PUT THE CAR IN TOP GEAR WITH IGNITION AND HAND-BRAKE OFF AND I'LL ROCK IT BACKWARDS AND FORWARDS TO FREE THE STARTER.

Engine turns slowly but won't start

Engine turns over but won't start — check blocked petrol filler

FRED, THE ENGINE WON'T START ALTHOUGH I FILLED UP AN HOUR AGO IN THE VILLAGE.
PERHAPS THE PETROL PUMP HAS PACKED UP...

Engine turns over but won't start — check the filter

Chapter 5

THE ENGINE WILL NOT RUN

Complete failure to show any signs of life by an engine when you try to start it is often due to an ignition fault. But failure to keep running, or hesitation as it runs, are more usually caused by trouble in the fuel system, between the petrol tank and the cylinder.

The job of the **carburettor,** the main component of the fuel system, is to change the liquid petrol in the fuel tank into an atomised mixture of fuel and air in the correct proportions. In its basic form the carburettor is similar to spray gun or a scent spray. As it emerges from the jet, the fuel is battered by the rushing air and breaks into tiny droplets so that a mist of air and fuel is produced. In order to move the air at a higher speed over the jet, the passageway through the carburettor is reduced in diameter near the jet. This is called the **choke** area. Since the same amount of air has to pass through a smaller hole in the same time its speed must increase to do so.

Controlling engine speed

To control the quantity of mixture that the cylinders can gulp in each inlet stroke, and so govern the speed of the engine, the **throttle,** a metal disc, is placed between the choke area and the cylinder port. When closed, the disc blocks off the passage through which mixture flows. When fully open, at full throttle, it is in line with the mixture flow.

The petrol is kept in a **tank** at the back of the car, usually below the rear seat or the boot floor, and has to be pumped up to the carburettor, which is mounted on the engine cylinder head. The **pump** is generally driven from the engine camshaft and has a filter gauze on the inlet side of a one-way valve leading to a chamber of which one wall is a diaphragm. This flexible diaphragm moves backwards and forwards to increase and decrease the chamber volume. As the volume increases petrol is drawn past the first one-way valve and as the volume decreases it is pushed past a second one-way valve to feed a constant-level device on the carburettor known as the **float chamber.**

In the feed to the float chamber is a valve moved by a float suspended in the petrol in the float chamber. As the petrol level rises, the float shuts the valve until, by usage, the petrol level drops. It is essential that the petrol level should remain just below the level of exit of the jet to obtain a correctly proportioned air/fuel mixture, and to stop petrol from dribbling out of the jet when the air flow is insufficient to mix all the fuel, such as when idling or when the engine is stopped.

Half a ton of air to one gallon of petrol

With a fixed diameter of choke and a fixed diameter of jet the engine would only get the proper balanced ratio of fuel and air at one speed. This ratio is around 1lb of petrol to 15lb of air or, in easier terms, about half a ton of air to a gallon of petrol. As the engine speed and, therefore, the mixture speed increases, the simple carburettor produces an increasingly richer mixture — one with too much fuel to too little air. There are two ways to compensate for this. Either by using a fuel well and compensating jet or by varying the size of the jet.

Fixed jet carburettors

With a fixed jet carburettor the **main jet,** which determines the maximum amount of fuel that can flow, is placed near the float chamber and is, in fact, a restriction in the feed to the jet at the choke area. Another feed passage from the float chamber also has a restriction of accurately predetermined size, the **compensating jet,** and this leads to an open-topped well on its way to a second jet in the choke area.

Fixed jet carburettor

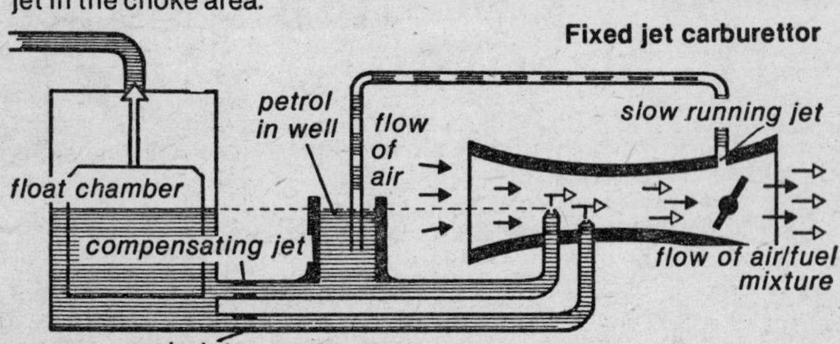

As the engine speeds up and more air rushes through the choke area trying to suck up more fuel, the main jet limits the amount of fuel available. The demand is made up by petrol from the well passing into the second jet. As the well empties during this acceleration period the rate at which it is refilled from the float chamber is restricted by the compensating jet, until the point is reached where the well is virtually empty and air is drawn into the second jet, thus keeping the overall mixture strength constant.

When the throttle is nearly shut across the main air/fuel passage, there is not enough suction on the jets to give a rich enough mixture for slow running conditions. However, the speed of the air through the small gap between the throttle edge and the passage wall is high and so a slow running jet is placed in this area. This jet is fed from a fuel passage that leads to a tube dipping into the petrol in the fuel well. When the engine speeds up the well level falls and petrol can no longer be sucked into the slow running jet thus, again, preventing too rich a mixture.

When starting a cold engine an even richer mixture is needed to compensate for fuel condensing on to the then cold walls of the multi-branched pipe, the inlet manifold, between the carburettor and the inlet ports in the cylinder head. This is provided by what is virtually a second small carburettor giving a very rich mixture and brought into use when the choke knob on the fascia is pulled.

Variable jet carburettors

The variable jet carburettor is a much simpler device and relies on a taper needle poking into the jet in the choke area. By moving the needle into or out of the jet, the flow of petrol can be controlled as the area between the bore of the jet and the needle varies. The needle is connected to a piston, or diaphragm, in a cylinder above the choke area. The area below the piston is open to atmospheric air pressure and the area above connected to suction in the choke area.

Variable jet carburettor

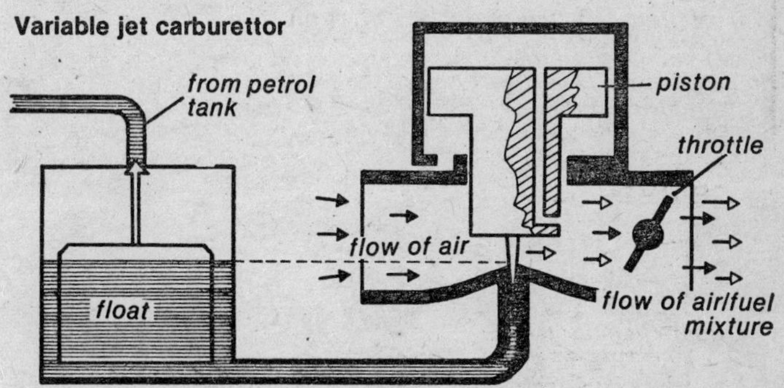

The underneath of the piston has a cylindrical extension of the same diameter as the choke area and when the piston is fully down this extension closes it off. When the engine begins to be turned with the starter, the suction of the inlet stroke in the closed off area on the engine side of the choke is fed to the top of the piston. This raises the piston and allows air to pass through the choke under the extension and over the top of the fuel jet to provide the air/fuel mixture. As the engine speed increases with the throttle opening, the differential pressures on the two sides of the piston cause the piston to rise and pull the needle further out of the jet to let more fuel flow.

In these variable jet carburettors the extra rich mixture for cold starting is provided either by moving the jet itself downwards and thus increasing the effective size of the petrol hole or by a separate small rich mixture starter carburettor.

Engine won't start but spits and bangs

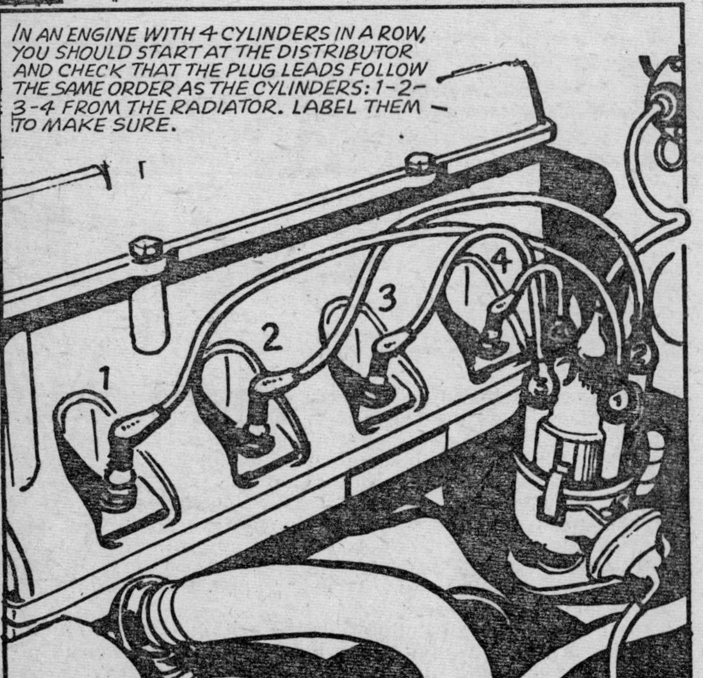

IN AN ENGINE WITH 4 CYLINDERS IN A ROW, YOU SHOULD START AT THE DISTRIBUTOR AND CHECK THAT THE PLUG LEADS FOLLOW THE SAME ORDER AS THE CYLINDERS: 1-2-3-4 FROM THE RADIATOR. LABEL THEM – TO MAKE SURE.

1
2
3
4

Engine hard to start when cold — check the plugs

Engine hard to start when cold — check the distributor

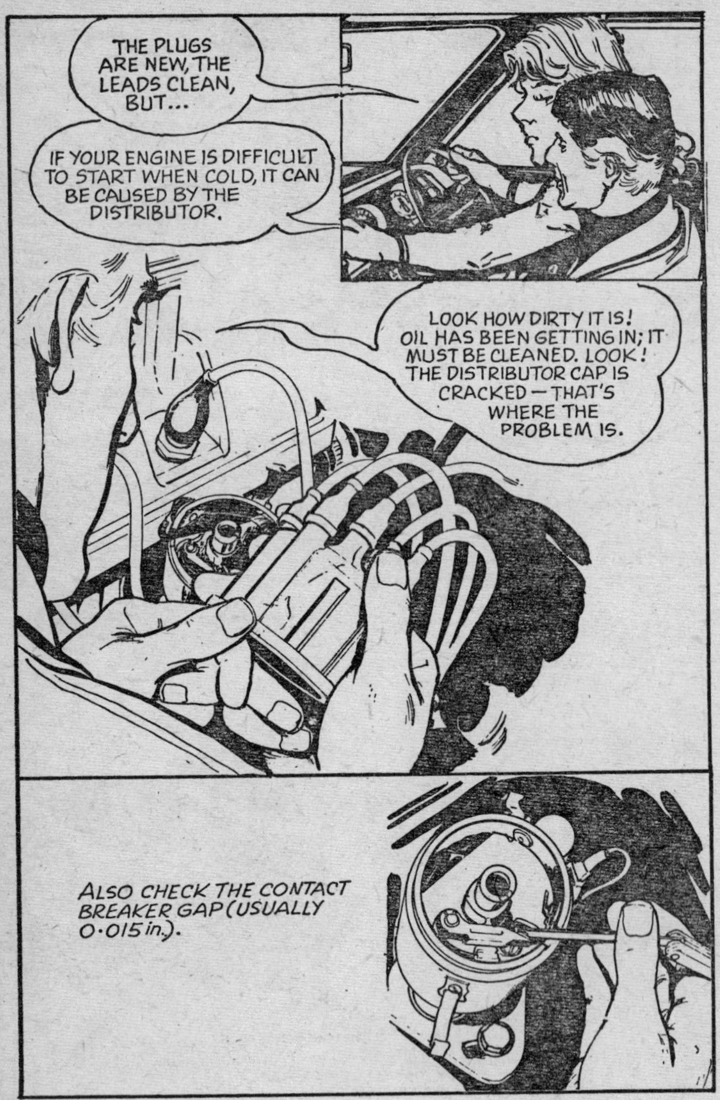

Engine hard to start when cold — check the choke

YES, BUT THE CABLE WHICH TURNS THE BUTTERFLY VALVE BLOCKING THE AIR INLET TO THE CARBURETTOR IS DISCONNECTED...

THE CABLE MUST BE RE-CONNECTED.

IF YOUR CAR IS EQUIPPED WITH AN AUTOMATIC CHOKE HAVE IT CHECKED BY A GARAGE.

Engine hard to start when cold — check the compression

... AND CHECK THE COMPRESSION TO MAKE SURE THERE'S NOT TOO MUCH WEAR IN THE *PISTONS* AND VALVES.

Engine flooded

Engine hard to start when hot — check for flooding

MAKE SURE THE CHOKE ISN'T OUT.

CHECK THAT THE FLOAT ISN'T PUNCTURED, AND THE JETS AREN'T BLOCKED. INCORRECT FLOAT LEVEL COULD CAUSE FLOODING.

Chapter 6

POOR RUNNING AND PERFORMANCE

Even though the engine starts and moves the car along the road, it may not do so as well as usual. It may proceed in fits and starts, or momentarily hesitate on acceleration. It may not have the power to ascend a particular hill in the usual gear or keep on boiling. These kinds of poor running are generally the result of various things getting out of adjustment and, of course, of pieces wearing out or breaking. To find out just what has gone wrong without taking the whole engine apart needs some logical thought and maybe a little detective thinking.

Listening for faults

Listening is the most effective way to begin a diagnosis. Does the hesitation, or the rattle, or other strange events, happen in synchronism with engine speed, *ie* increase in frequency with increasing engine speed, irrespective of road speed or gear engaged? If not, the trouble is probably not in the engine.

Mechanical trouble

Does the sound of something wrong correspond to the engine speed and remain steady in that it is happening with every revolution of the engine? This is a sign of a mechanical trouble, such as the tappets needing adjustment or something that has broken loose. A rattling sound when the engine is cold together with an increase in oil consumption can mean worn pistons.

Plugs and valves

If the engine is running regularly, but it is down on power and does not sound as well as usual, drip a drop of water into each of the exhaust pipes, where they meet the cylinder head, and note if one of the drops lasts longer than the others. If by this test you can see that one cylinder is cooler than the others, it is likely the sparking plug is not working properly, or the valves of that cylinder are leaking.

Electrical faults

Broadly speaking if the poor running is sharply intermittent and not particularly dependent upon engine speed, it is likely to be the ignition system at fault. Look for perished insulation in the HT leads from the coil to the distributor and from the distributor to the sparking plugs. Clean the outside insulation of the plugs and look for black marks on the coil and distributor cover insulation that show the spark voltage is tracking along a dirt path that is easier than jumping the plug gap.

Fuel system faults

If, on the other hand, the poor running is a loss of performance or a hesitation when accelerating or rough running at slow engine speeds the trouble is likely to be in the fuel system between the tank and the inlet manifold. Small drops of water can partially or temporarily block fuel filters and can lift into a jet when the fuel flow is high and fall away when the flow decreases. Loss of top end performance may be caused by a blocking of the main jet since it is only then that this jet is really effective. Hesitation on acceleration could be blockage of the compensating jet, or trouble with the carburettor pump that provides extra fuel for acceleration power in fixed jet carburettors. Low engine speed hesitancy may be in the slow running system jet, or caused by the choke not being fully stopped when the knob has been pushed home, resulting in a mixture that is too rich for a warmed-up engine.

Engine runs too fast

Engine misfires when idling — check the carburettor

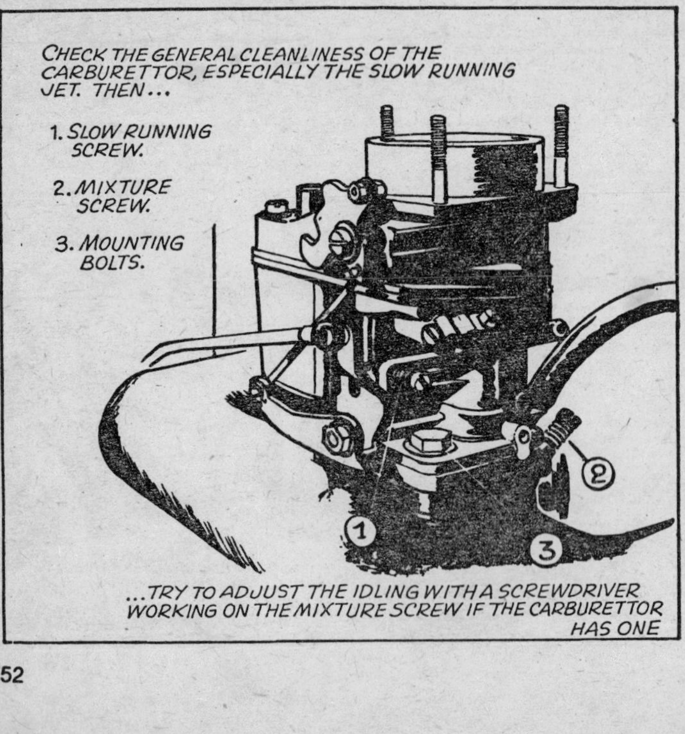

CHECK THE GENERAL CLEANLINESS OF THE CARBURETTOR, ESPECIALLY THE SLOW RUNNING JET. THEN...

1. SLOW RUNNING SCREW.
2. MIXTURE SCREW.
3. MOUNTING BOLTS.

1
2
3

...TRY TO ADJUST THE IDLING WITH A SCREWDRIVER WORKING ON THE MIXTURE SCREW IF THE CARBURETTOR HAS ONE

Engine misfires when idling — check the distributor

I CAN'T SEEM TO GET THE SLOW RUNNING RIGHT, FRED. BUT THE CARBURETTOR SEEMS TO BE O.K.

WHAT'S UP, JOHN?

Poor running when hot

I ADVISE YOU TO GET IT CHANGED, THAT'S EASIEST – ALTHOUGH MOST GARAGES CAN CHECK THE COIL OUTPUT.

Engine misfires when idling — check compression

Poor performance, high fuel consumption — check vacuum advance

Chapter 7

THE ESSENTIAL FLUIDS

Oil and water are both essential to the running of an engine. Oil both lubricates and cools the moving parts, while water is circulated inside the engine block to cool it.

The cooling system

With all the flame and fury that is happening inside the cylinders a lot of heat is produced. If this heat were allowed to build up it would eventually cause a lot of damage to the inside of the engine. The top of the piston would start to melt and the seatings for the valves, that prevent the gases getting out at the wrong time, would become pitted and cracked and cease to seal.

To keep the engine cool, the cylinder block is formed as four, or however many cylinders there are, tubes held inside a rectangular tank. Similarly the cylinder head has the combustion spaces and the inlet and exhaust parts sealed into another tank-like casing. These two tanks, or coolant spaces, are connected together by holes in the two flat faces where they are bolted together and are full of water.

Circulating water round the engine

The coolant is circulated by a **water pump** belt driven from a pulley on the end of the crankshaft, that takes colder water from the bottom of a radiator and pushes it round through the cylinder block and cylinder head to the top of the radiator. The radiator consists of a large number of thin rectangular section tubes set vertically between top and bottom tanks. These tubes present as great an area as possible to the air blowing through the radiator as the car moves. To keep the cooling flow of air at low speeds an engine-driven fan is fitted behind the radiator, often on the pulley on the water pump shaft. Most modern cars have an electrically driven fan switched on when the water gets hot by a thermostat switch in the top tank of the radiator.

Warming up the engine

To help the engine warm up rapidly to its best working temperature, a thermostatically controlled valve is fitted in the top water connection between the cylinder head and the radiator. This thermostat has metal bellows that expand as the water gets hotter and open the valve to allow full flow through the system.

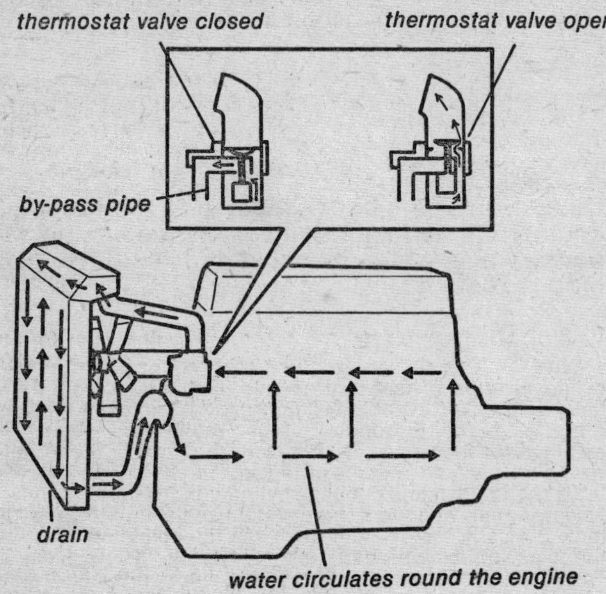

Cooling system

Water under pressure

Since the most efficient temperature for the engine to work is around the boiling temperature of the cooling water, the normal boiling point is raised by slightly pressurizing the system. This allows the system to run up to 100°C or just over without boiling the water away. To get the pressurisation the radiator filler cap seals the radiator and has a spring-loaded safety valve that vents into an overflow pipe if the pressure gets too high.

As water expands when it is heated, the radiator should never be filled above the mark on the tank, or the level quoted in the instruction book. If it is overfilled, the water will be blown out of the overflow and be lost along with the **anti-freeze** it contains.

If the engine overheats

If an engine boils and steam comes from the overflow, stop as soon as you can and let the engine cool down before you do anything. If you try and take off the radiator filler cap you will get a geyser of boiling water in your face! You can help to cool the system by running the heater and its fan.

The lubrication system

To keep the many metal surfaces on the moving parts of the engine from rubbing on each other and wearing out too fast, a film of oil is maintained between them. Some of these surfaces are lightly loaded and can exist with oil that splashes around inside the engine, but other heavily loaded surfaces need the oil to be pumped between them.

The oil reservoir is the sump forming the bottom of the crankcase and from there the oil is sucked through a coarse filter by an engine-driven **oil pump** that delivers pressurised oil to the many engine bearings.

Why change the oil filter?

From the pump the oil passes through a fine **filter** in a metal canister on the side of the crankcase. This canister contains a porous paper element that traps any dirt or grit or metal particles that may be in the oil and would otherwise damage the smooth bearing surfaces. If this filter becomes choked because it has not been changed at the proper intervals, a relief valve in the canister will open and allow unfiltered oil to flow round the engine. So make sure the filter is changed as often as necessary.

The filtered oil is pumped to the main crankshaft bearings in the crankcase and passes through holes in the bearings and the crakshaft to the bearings for the connecting rod and the big end bearings. The top connecting rod bearing in the piston and the piston and cylinder walls rely on oil splashing out from the crankshaft. Another feed from the oil pump goes to lubricate the valve rocker bearings and to spray over the cams and the valve stems. Eventually all the oil drains back down inside the engine and is collected in the sump ready to go round again.

Oil as a coolant

As well as lubrication, the oil has another function — that of helping cool the internal parts of the engine. It picks up heat as it moves round the moving parts and when it returns to the sump it has a chance to cool off, as the bottom of the sump has a large area exposed to the cold air blowing under the car. If the oil level is allowed to get too low the oil does not get time to cool. Because the oil gets hotter it thins out and does not work as well to keep the moving surfaces apart.

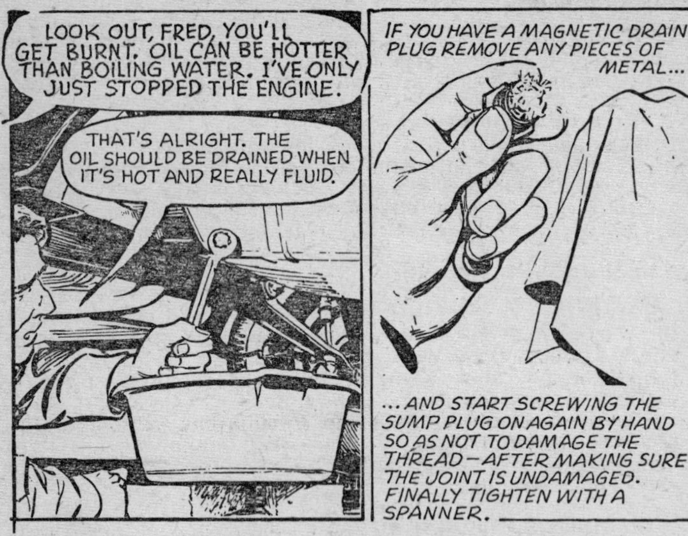

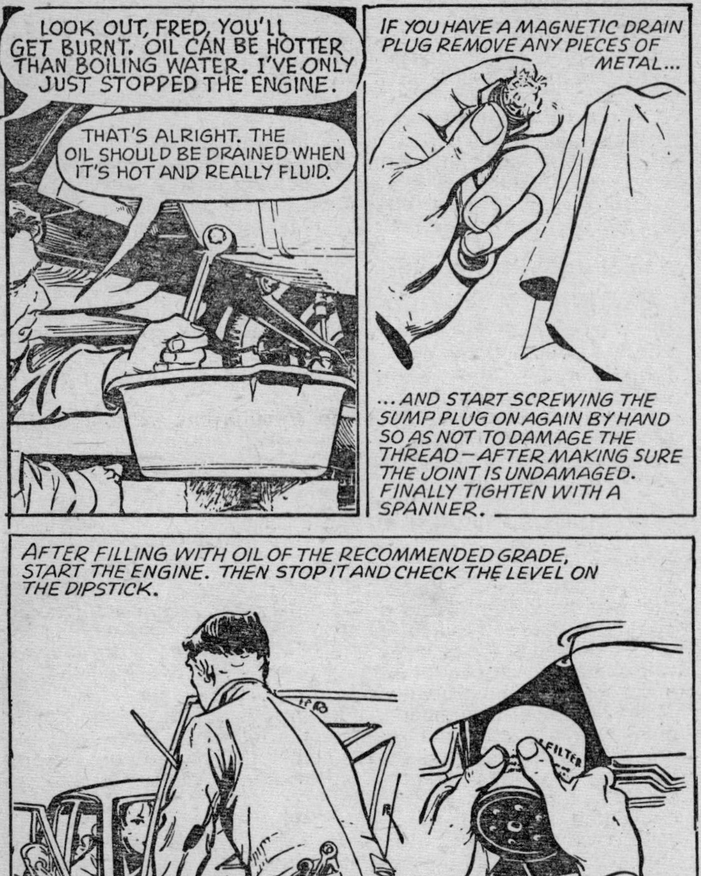

AFTER FILLING WITH OIL OF THE RECOMMENDED GRADE, START THE ENGINE. THEN STOP IT AND CHECK THE LEVEL ON THE DIPSTICK.

FILTER

CHANGE THE OIL FILTER AT THE INTERVALS SHOWN IN THE HAND-BOOK — USUALLY 3,000 OR 6,000 MILES.

Poor performance, high fuel consumption — check air filter

Engine overheating — check the cooling system

Engine uses too much water

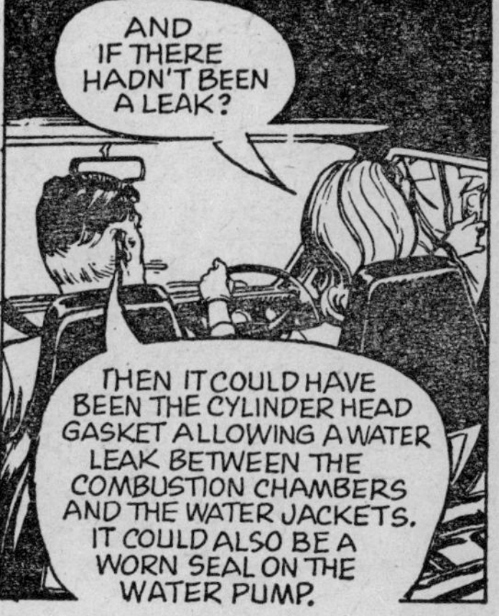

Engine uses too much oil — check for leaks

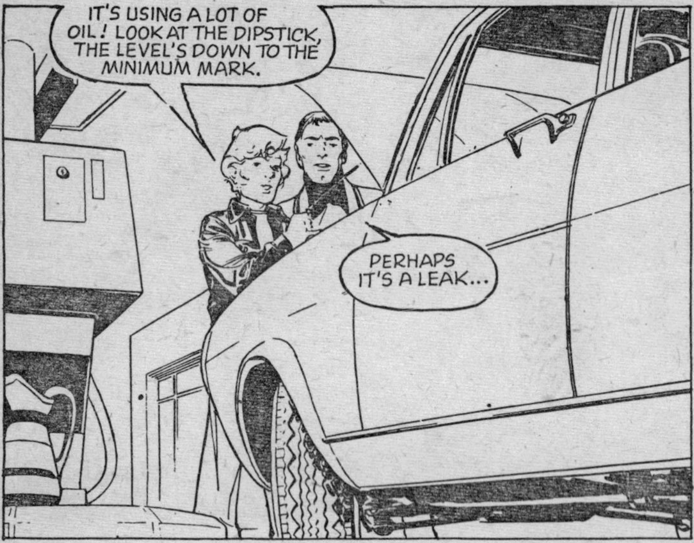

IT'S USING A LOT OF OIL! LOOK AT THE DIPSTICK, THE LEVEL'S DOWN TO THE MINIMUM MARK.

PERHAPS IT'S A LEAK...

Engine uses too much oil — check for burning oil

Oil level rising in the sump

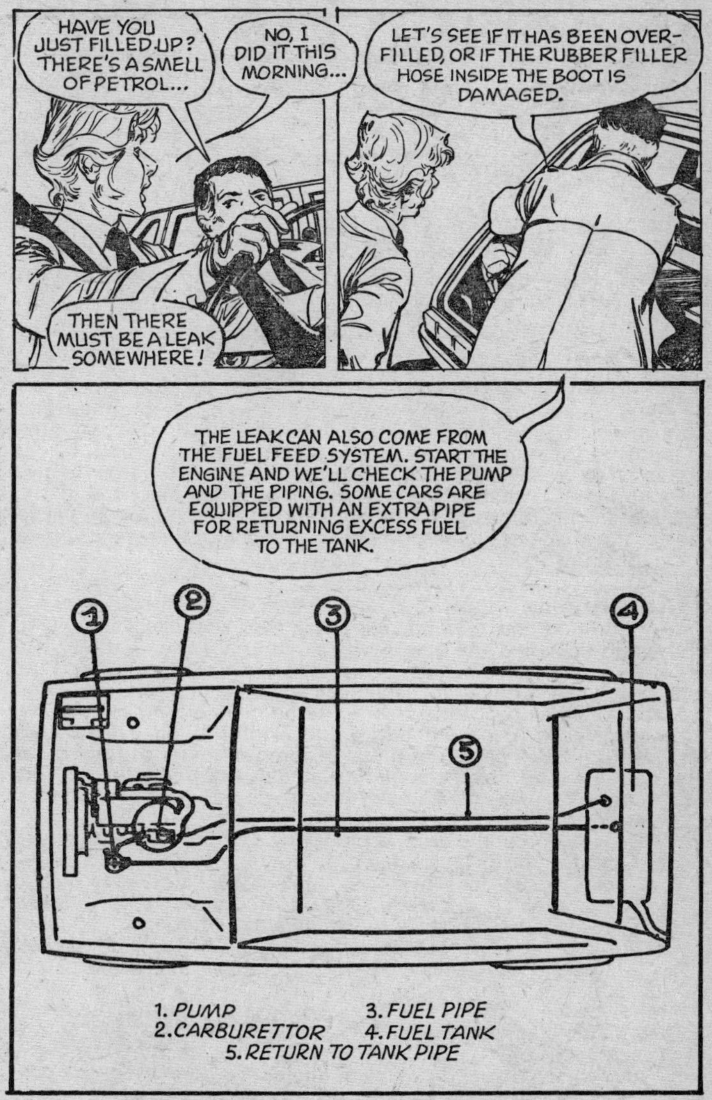
HAVE YOU JUST FILLED UP? THERE'S A SMELL OF PETROL...
NO, I DID IT THIS MORNING...
THEN THERE MUST BE A LEAK SOMEWHERE!
LET'S SEE IF IT HAS BEEN OVER-FILLED, OR IF THE RUBBER FILLER HOSE INSIDE THE BOOT IS DAMAGED.
THE LEAK CAN ALSO COME FROM THE FUEL FEED SYSTEM. START THE ENGINE AND WE'LL CHECK THE PUMP AND THE PIPING. SOME CARS ARE EQUIPPED WITH AN EXTRA PIPE FOR RETURNING EXCESS FUEL TO THE TANK.
1
2
3
4
5
1. PUMP
2. CARBURETTOR
3. FUEL PIPE
4. FUEL TANK
5. RETURN TO TANK PIPE

Chapter 8

STOPPING AND STEERING

Tyres and brakes are perhaps the two most important parts of the car. Your safety depends on them. They should be checked regularly, and if you understand how they work, you can check more easily if they are up to standard.

The brakes

Just as the heat energy stored in the petrol is turned into movement energy to get the mass of the car moving, so must the energy of the moving mass be translated back into heat if the car is to be slowed. This is done by rubbing two parts together to give friction that produces heat, which is lost to the surrounding air. There are two types of friction-producing devices in use, called after the shape of the part that goes round with the wheel. These are the **drum brake** and the **disc brake.**

Drum brakes

The drum of the drum brake is a relatively shallow cylinder with one end open and the other end closed by an integral end plate bolted to the hub that carries the road wheel. The outside of the drum is usually ribbed for increased stiffness and to provide fins for better cooling. The inside is very smooth and gives the surface on which other parts press to produce the friction. These other parts are curved pieces of metal covered on most of their outer surfaces with a special friction material, **the brake lining.** This material is mainly asbestos to stand up to the heat, bonded together with brass wire and glues called resins.

The open end of the drum is closed by a circular plate, the **back plate,** fixed to the axle part that does not go round with the wheel. The back plate carries a **pivot pin,** against which one end of each curved metal piece, the **brake shoes,** rest. Diametrically opposite the pivot pin is a bearing for the spindle of a rectangular piece of metal, the **brake cam,** that lies between the other ends of the two brake shoes. The two shoes are pulled together onto the pivot and cam and away from the interior of the drum by springs, which stretch between them. The other end of the cam spindle has a lever that is connected to the **brake pedal** or **hand brake lever** by a cable.

When the brake cable is pulled, the lever rotates the brake cam to force the ends of the shoes apart and press the friction linings

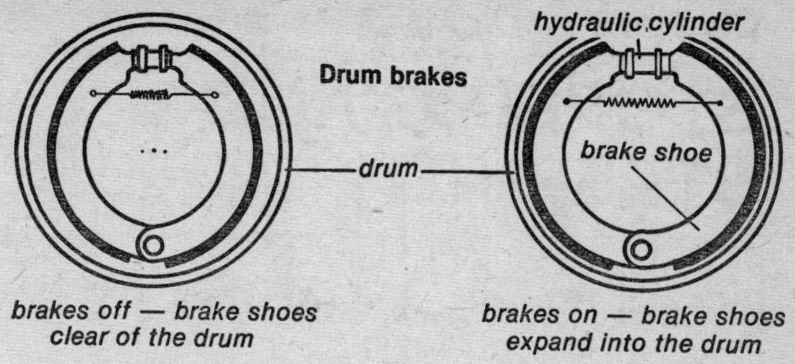

brakes off — brake shoes clear of the drum

brakes on — brake shoes expand into the drum

against the brake drum interior. This produces friction that slows or stops the wheel.

Since all the wheels are moving up and down on the suspension system and the front wheels have to steer, cable operation is at a disadvantage. To overcome this, the brake cam is replaced by a piston and cylinder that will expand between the shoe ends when **hydraulic pressure** is applied within the cylinder. This pressure is produced by another piston, connected to the brake pedal, working in a cylinder fixed to the floor in front of the pedals. This latter cylinder is the **master cylinder** and pressure from it is taken to the **slave cylinders** in the brake drums by a series of rigid and flexible pipes.

Maintaining hydraulics

This system works because the pressure in a liquid is always the same at all places. Thus, if pressing on the pedal moves the master cylinder piston to produce a pressure of X pounds per square inch, then all the slave cylinders will also have X psi pushing their pistons to expand the brake shoes. If there is the smallest air bubble in the hydraulic system, the pressure will squeeze the bubble elastically and the brakes will have a spongy feel and can fail altogether. Hence the need to keep the brake fluid reservoir full and to bleed the air out of the system if any should get in.

Disc brakes

Drum brakes have the disadvantages that friction material dust, produced as the linings wear, and water get trapped in the drum and that the hottest points are inside the drum out through which the heat has to escape.

In a disc brake, the drum is replaced by a relatively thin disc and the friction material takes the form of two **friction pads,** on opposite sides of the disc. These pads are acted on by pistons in cylinders formed in a U-shaped caliper that enfolds the edge of the disc. The caliper is fixed to the axle and takes the place of the stationary back plate. The pistons are moved by hydraulic pressure from a pedal master cylinder to clamp the pads against the disc sides.

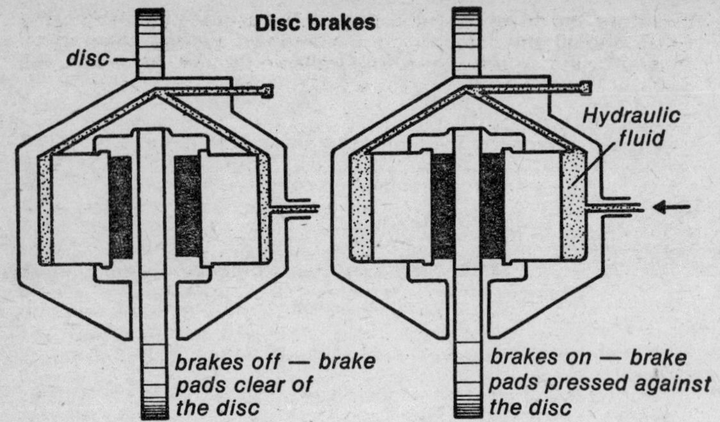

As the disc is out in the open air and the greater part of its area is not shrouded by the caliper and pads, the disc can dissipate much more heat to the surrounding air. Moreover, water and friction material dust is thrown off by centrifugal action or wiped away by the leading edges of the pads. A further benefit is the ease with which pads can be examined for wear, and replaced, compared with the more complicated job of taking drums off to get at the linings on the shoes.

Vacuum servo unit

With the increase in speeds and weights of cars, the amount of pedal pressure needed to stop increased until it became almost impossible, except for the strong, to get full braking force. This has been dealt with by the use of a device known as a **brake vacuum servo unit.**

The servo unit is mounted in the hydraulic pipeline between the master cylinder and the junction of the separate pipes to the four brake cylinders. As the brake pedal is depressed, the pressure from the master cylinder goes through the system and at the same time opens an air valve in the servo unit. Air from the atmosphere goes through this valve and acts on one side of a flexible diaphragm arranged across the centre of a closed cylindrical chamber. The other side is connected to the carburettor on the engine side of the throttle to provide a vacuum on the other side of the diaphragm.

The pressure difference between the atmosphere and suction is somewhere around 10 or 12lb per square inch and, as this pressure is acting on a diaphragm some eight inches in diameter, a considerable force is produced. A piston rod at the diaphragm centre takes this force to increase the pressure in the hydraulic fluid working the brakes and so reduce the pedal pressure needed. The valves are designed such that the increase in pressure is proportional to the pressure produced by the master cylinder and, therefore, the driver has full control of the degree of braking being used. Should any defect occur in the servo system, the original master cylinder pressure is still available though, of course, the pedal pressure required to stop will be higher.

Dual brake circuits

A drawback of the hydraulic system is that if there is a leak anywhere the pressure cannot be built up to work the brakes. Thus if a pipe breaks or becomes disconnected the whole system fails immediately and leaves the car brakeless, except for the separate handbrake. For the last few years new cars have been fitted with a dual circuit system in which two wheels are braked from one circuit and the other two from a second separate circuit, the only common part being the master cylinder and part of the vacuum servo unit. By this means, failure in one circuit will still leave half the wheels braked, which is much better than nothing.

Tyres

The tyres are probably the most important parts of a car for they are the only link with the road surface. They have to provide traction grip for driving the car, traction grip for stopping it, sideways grip for steering and to cushion the car, and its occupants, against the smaller bumps.

The air in the tyres has the double duty of acting as part of the springing system and to keep the tyre in the right shape so that the tread pattern remains efficient. Too low a pressure of air will not keep the tread blocks separated enough for proper grip, especially when they have to clear surface water away to let the rubber grip. Too high a pressure will prevent enough tread meeting the road where the tyre flattens and also make the tyre too bouncy so that grip can, again, be lost.

To reinforce the tyre and help the tread keep its proper shape there are plies of fabric, or metal, embedded in the carcase. There are two ways of arranging this reinforcement, **crossply** and **radial ply.**

Types of tyres

In a crossply tyre the fabric, which is nearly all warp or longitudinal threads, is arranged so that the threads are tangential to the wheel rim and as they extend from both sides they cross each other more or less at right angles. Hence the name of cross ply.

The radial ply tyre has its plies arranged so that the threads are radial to the wheel rim and therefore run straight across inside the carcase from one side to the other. This makes the tyre much more flexible in its walls. To stiffen the tread area belts of fabric or metal plies run round the circumference under the tread and these, being inextensible, keep the tread pattern stable.

Due to the difference in wall stiffness and other factors these two kinds of tyres have different handling characteristics and must not be mixed on one axle. If two tyres are one kind and the other two of the other kind, the radial ply tyres must always be on the two back wheels. The wording on the tyre walls will always say if it is a radial ply tyre.

Tyre pressures

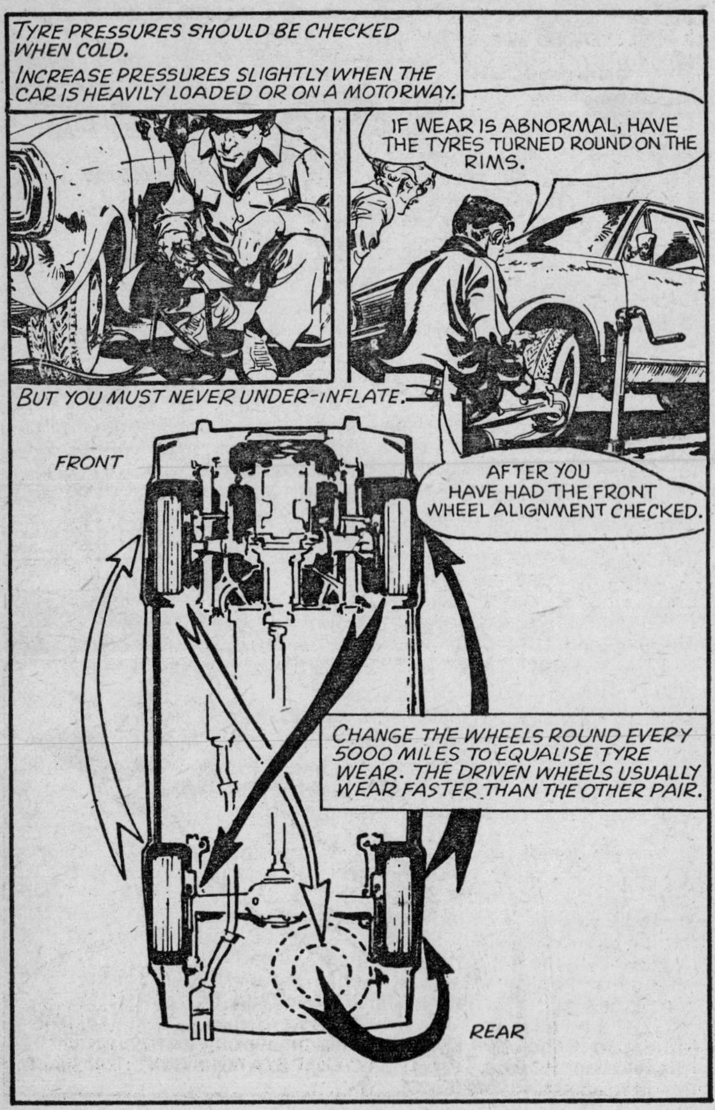

Steering wheel vibrations

Poor roadholding — check shock absorbers

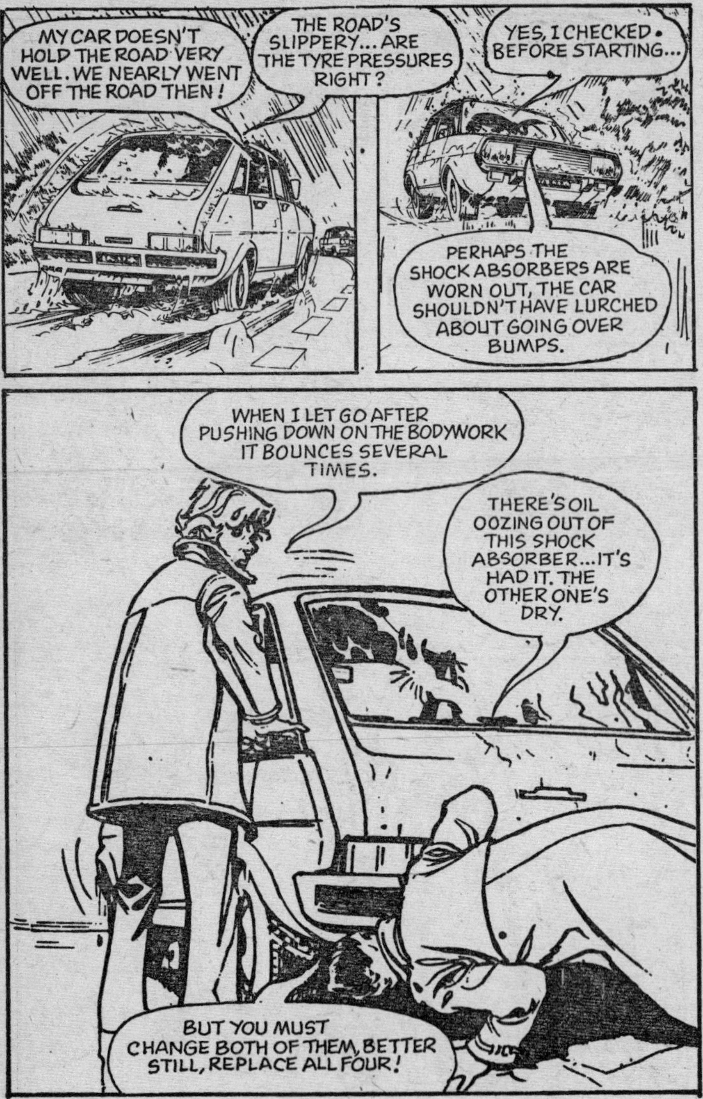

WHEN I LET GO AFTER PUSHING DOWN ON THE BODYWORK IT BOUNCES SEVERAL TIMES.

THERE'S OIL OOZING OUT OF THIS SHOCK ABSORBER... IT'S HAD IT. THE OTHER ONE'S DRY.

BUT YOU MUST CHANGE BOTH OF THEM, BETTER STILL, REPLACE ALL FOUR!

Poor roadholding — check suspension

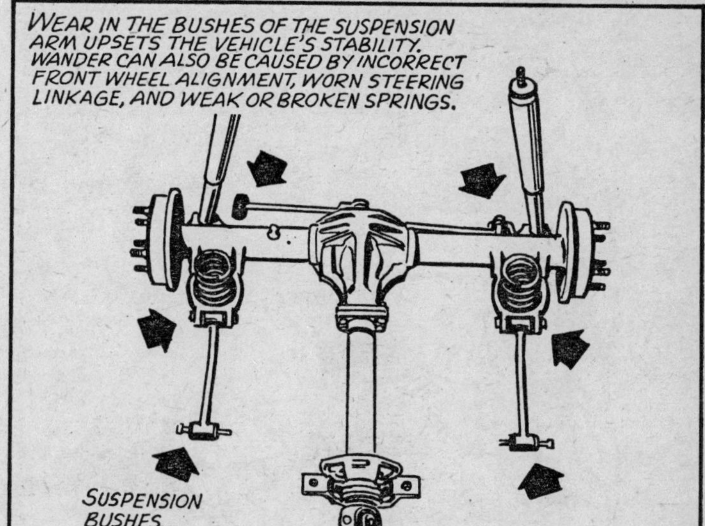

WEAR IN THE BUSHES OF THE SUSPENSION ARM UPSETS THE VEHICLE'S STABILITY. WANDER CAN ALSO BE CAUSED BY INCORRECT FRONT WHEEL ALIGNMENT, WORN STEERING LINKAGE, AND WEAK OR BROKEN SPRINGS.

SUSPENSION BUSHES.

The car pulls to one side

DO YOU THINK IT NEEDS CHANGING, FRED?
YES, YOU'RE BREAKING THE LAW! TYRE TREAD MUSTN'T BE LESS THAN 1mm. IN DEPTH.
IS IT DANGEROUS?
AND HOW! IN RAIN, WATER CANNOT DRAIN AWAY IF THERE IS LITTLE TREAD AND THE TYRE LOSES CONTACT WITH THE ROAD. IT'S CALLED AQUAPLANING.
BESIDES, THE SIDEWALL IS CUT AND THERE'S A NASTY BULGE.
AT LEAST I WON'T NEED TO CHANGE THAT TYRE – IT'S ALRIGHT.
I'M NOT SO SURE... THE RIM IS DENTED, WHICH MEANS YOU'VE PROBABLY HIT THE KERB. THE SIDEWALL FABRIC OF THE TYRE MAY HAVE BEEN DAMAGED. IT MUST BE TAKEN OFF AND INSPECTED.

Tyre wear — check wheel alignment

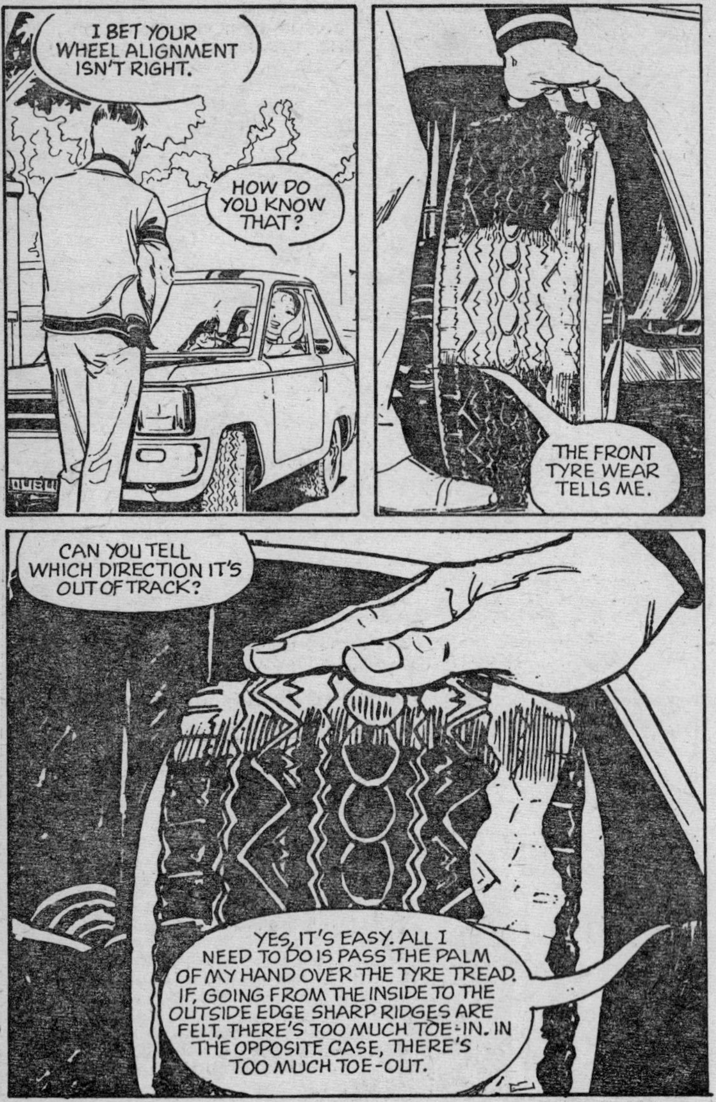

CAN YOU TELL WHICH DIRECTION IT'S OUT OF TRACK?

YES, IT'S EASY. ALL I NEED TO DO IS PASS THE PALM OF MY HAND OVER THE TYRE TREAD. IF, GOING FROM THE INSIDE TO THE OUTSIDE EDGE SHARP RIDGES ARE FELT, THERE'S TOO MUCH TOE-IN. IN THE OPPOSITE CASE, THERE'S TOO MUCH TOE-OUT.

Tyre wear — check the tread

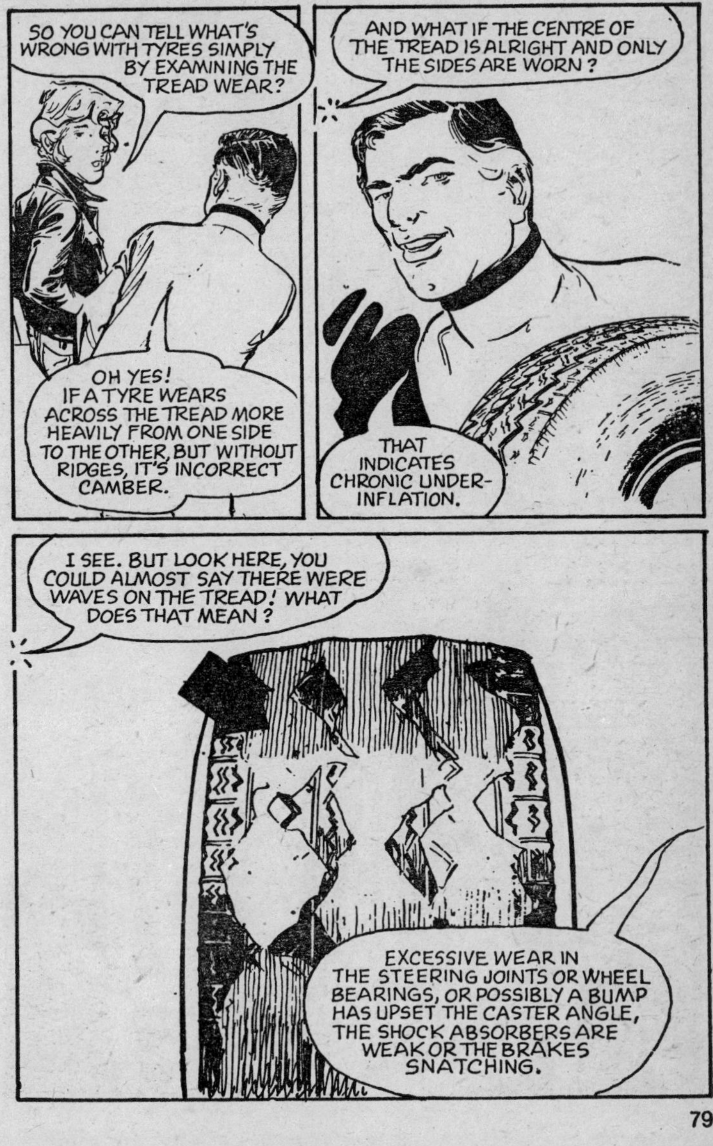

I SEE. BUT LOOK HERE, YOU COULD ALMOST SAY THERE WERE WAVES ON THE TREAD! WHAT DOES THAT MEAN?

EXCESSIVE WEAR IN THE STEERING JOINTS OR WHEEL BEARINGS, OR POSSIBLY A BUMP HAS UPSET THE CASTER ANGLE, THE SHOCK ABSORBERS ARE WEAK OR THE BRAKES SNATCHING.

The car pulls to one side when braking

Brakes fade when hot

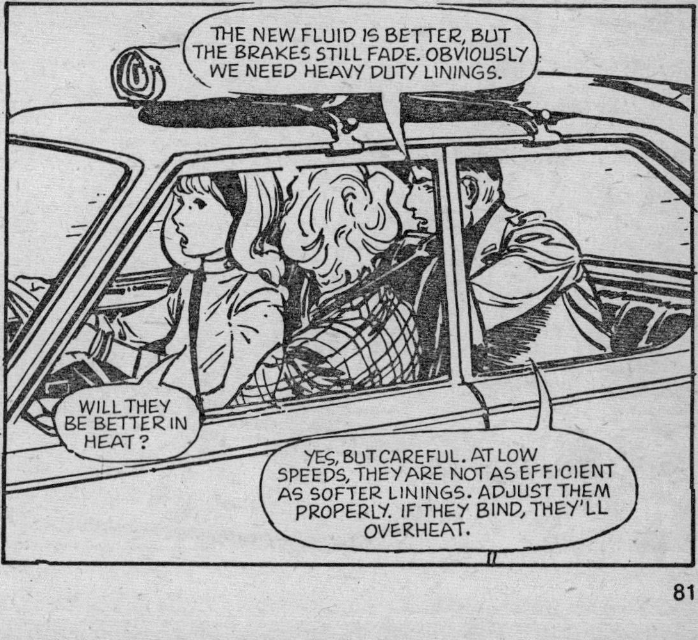

THE NEW FLUID IS BETTER, BUT THE BRAKES STILL FADE. OBVIOUSLY WE NEED HEAVY DUTY LININGS.

WILL THEY BE BETTER IN HEAT?

YES, BUT CAREFUL. AT LOW SPEEDS, THEY ARE NOT AS EFFICIENT AS SOFTER LININGS. ADJUST THEM PROPERLY. IF THEY BIND, THEY'LL OVERHEAT.

Spongy brake pedal

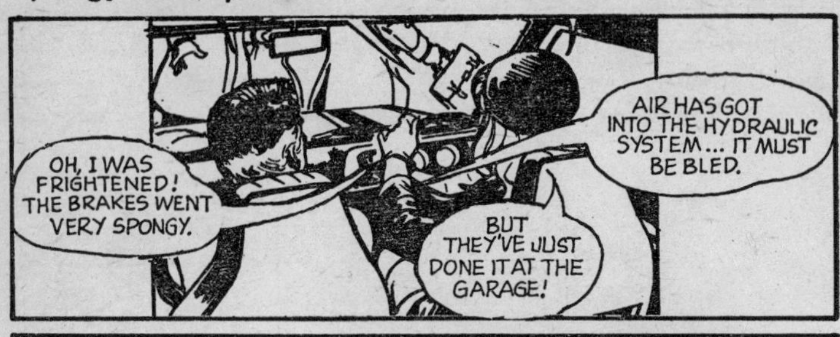

Soft brake pedal

HEY, FRED, MY BRAKE PEDAL IS VERY SOFT. IT FEELS AS IF IT GOES TO THE FLOOR.

LISTEN, JOHN...

SIT AT THE WHEEL, PUSH AS HARD AS YOU CAN ON THE PEDAL UNTIL IT FEELS HARD...

Back wheels lock up

Brake servo efficiency

Chapter 9

MECHANICAL TROUBLE

The rest of the mechanical parts of the car make up the transmission that takes the power from the engine flywheel to the two driving road wheels. This comprises the clutch, the gearbox and the final drive.

The Clutch

The clutch has the double duty of disengaging the engine from the road wheels and of acting as a low speed gearbox. If it were not for the first use the engine would have to be restarted each time there was a traffic hold up. Once the engine had been started, unless the bottom gear ratio was incredibly low, the power available would not be enough to move the car off, particularly on a hill. The ability of the clutch to slip, so that the driving and driven parts turn at different speeds and still transmit a turning force, torque, lets the car move off smoothly.

The friction clutch is rather like a sandwich in which the meat part is a disc covered on both sides with friction material and the bread parts are, on one side the rear face of the **flywheel,** and on the other a flat ring called the **pressure plate.** The pressure plate is carried in a clutch cover bolted to the flywheel. It is connected to the cover by thin flexible strips that let the pressure plate move backwards and forwards, at the same time making sure that the plate rotates with the cover. When the flywheel and cover are rotating these strips pull the pressure plate with them.

The clutch plate, has on each face rings of the same friction material as used for the brakes. It is clamped between the flywheel and pressure plate by a slightly dished plate spring called a **diaphragm spring.**

When the clutch pedal is not being used, the spring forces the pressure plate forward to clamp the clutch plate to the flywheel, and thus everything goes round together. Through the centre of the clutch plate is a serrated hole fitting over a similarly serrated shaft that is the power input shaft to the gearbox. These two sets of serrations, called splines, allow the plate to move axially along the shaft and at the same time remain in driving connection.

Clutch mechanism

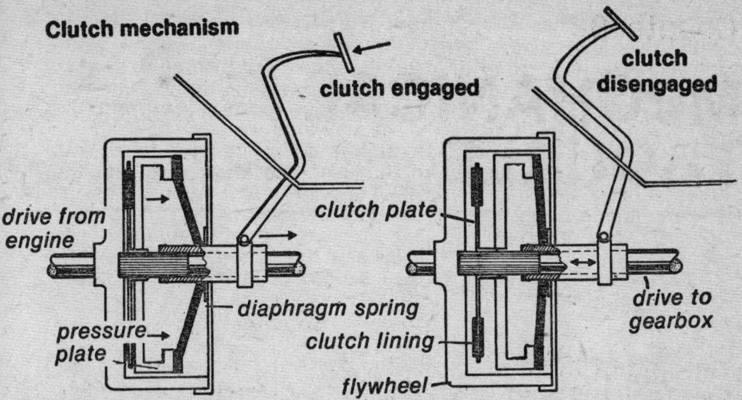

Pressing on the pedal causes a ball bearing to move forwards to act on the diaphragm. The spring flexes and moves the pressure plate away from the flywheel face. This unclamps the clutch plate, thus releasing the drive to the gearbox. Less than full travel of the clutch pedal results in less than all of the spring clamping force being removed and so the clutch plate is dragged round by the friction of the flywheel and pressure plate. The amount of dragging is proportional to the amount of spring pressure not removed by pedal movement. Thus the clutch plate and gearbox shaft can be rotating more slowly than the flywheel and at the same time transmit some torque. Slowly releasing the pedal gently increases the spring pressure on the plate and this increases the amount of torque that is transmitted and away moves the car without jerk or snatch.

The Gearbox

Since the speed range of the road wheels is much greater than that of the engine and the engine delivers its greatest turning force, or torque, at around two thirds of its full speed, there is a need to vary the gearing between engine and wheels. It is the job of the gearbox to provide a selection of gear ratios to suit driving conditions.

The gearbox is a light alloy box containing two parallel shafts, the **main shaft** and the **layshaft**. The mainshaft is in two pieces — the gearbox **input shaft**, that carries the clutch plate, and the gearbox **output shaft** that takes the drive out to the driving wheels.

The inner end of the input shaft is formed as a gear. At the back end of this gear are a set of clutching teeth, like stubby gear teeth, and in the centre is a roller bearing. The front end of the output shaft part of the main shaft is carried in this bearing and the shaft has two sets of rectangular grooves, splines, that provide a positive drive to two internally splined rings that can slide along the shaft splines. Behind and between the two sets of splines are bearings for two freely rotatable gears.

The layshaft has four different size gears all made in one piece with the shaft. The largest of these gears has its teeth permanently meshed with the teeth of the input mainshaft gear so that, as long as the clutch is engaged, the engine is always turning the layshaft. The other three gears engage tooth-to-tooth with the free gears on the output part of the mainshaft.

The free mainshaft gears are all formed on their end faces with clutch teeth, dogs, similar to those on the input gear and the splined rings have a second set of larger internal splines that can engage these dogs when the rings are moved along the shaft towards an appropriate free gear. The sleeves are moved axially by semi-circular forks fitting in grooves on the outside of the sleeves. The forks are fixed to longitudinal selector rods that can be moved by the gear lever.

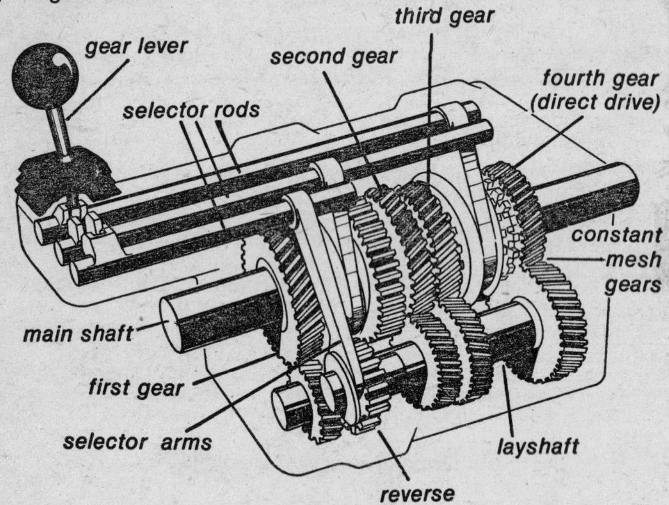

Gearbox — *four speed and reverse*

The **selector rods** have grooves in their ends furthest from the **selector forks,** so that when the gear lever is rocked to one side it engages the groove of one rod. Backwards and forwards gear lever movement moves the fork and ring of one free gear pair along the mainshaft to make the appropriate ring splines engage with the dogs of that gear. When the splines and dogs are engaged that gear becomes drivingly fixed to the main shaft. Since the input shaft gear is driving the layshaft and a layshaft gear is driving the engaged gear there is a drive, at a reduced speed, from input to output shafts.

Movement of the gear lever and selector rod in the other fore and aft direction will produce engagement of the other gear of the pair and sideways gear lever movement will allow engagement of two further gear ratios. This gives four forward gears. Reverse gear is arranged by yet another selector rod that moves a small gear on a separate shaft to engage between a layshaft gear and a mainshaft gear. This small gear changes the direction of rotation of the mainshaft gear and produces reverse.

For top gear, the front splined ring engages the dog teeth on the end of the input gear so that the two parts of the mainshaft are drivingly locked together to run at the same speed or direct drive.

Synchromesh

Since the splines and dogs can only engage smoothly when they are rotating at the same speed, a synchronising mechanism is built in to the sliding rings. The outer part of the ring is made separate from the inner part and the two are splined together. The outer part moves the inner through a spring loaded ball in one part engaging a groove in the other part. When the ring is moved by the selector fork both parts begin to move together until a tapered hole on the inner part meets a similarly tapered cone on the gear. At this point the internal splines have just not reached the gear dog teeth. The two conical surfaces touch to begin to rotate the gear by friction and when the gear has reached the speed of the sleeve the outer part can continue its travel to engage the splines and dogs without a crunch. This is the synchromesh mechanism.

Sychromesh unit

Final Drive

The gearbox output is taken to the final drive unit directly in a front wheel drive car, or through a long tubular shaft, the **propeller shaft**, on a rear wheel drive car. The final gear drive has a pair of bevel gears that turn the drive through a right angle so that the north/south engine and gearbox can drive an east/west axle. These gears are different sizes to give a reduction ratio of around five to one, because the engine runs much faster than the road wheels need to rotate. The final drive also includes a **differential**, or balance, gearing that still provides an equal distribution of torque to the two wheels even though they must turn at different speeds when the car goes round a corner.

Engine noisy — check tappets

Engine pinks — check petrol grade

FRED, ARE YOU PLAYING MARBLES?
NOT EXACTLY!
I'M LOOKING AT THE STEAM COMING FROM YOUR EXHAUST; IT'S NOT RIGHT, THE ENGINE IS QUITE HOT.
IT'S BECAUSE IT'S COLD!
ALL THE SAME, CHECK THE WATER LEVEL IN THE RADIATOR. THE STEAM SHOWS YOUR ENGINE'S USING TOO MUCH WATER.
NOW THE ENGINE'S COLD, I'M TIGHTENING THE CYLINDER HEAD. IF THE WATER CONSUMPTION GOES ON LIKE THIS, GET THE HEAD GASKET CHECKED.

Smell of hot gas inside — check exhaust manifold

SEE THAT THE EXHAUST MANIFOLD BOLTS ARE TIGHT. CHECK THERE ARE NO CRACKS IN THE EXHAUST SYSTEM.

THAT THE MANIFOLD EXHAUST PIPE JOINT ISN'T LEAKING. DON'T DRIVE THE CAR, FIX IT RIGHT AWAY.

Diagnosis by the colour of the spark plug

THE COLOUR OF THE DEPOSITS ON THE NOSE OF THE PLUG GIVES VERY PRECISE INDICATIONS OF THE CONDITION OF THE ENGINE.

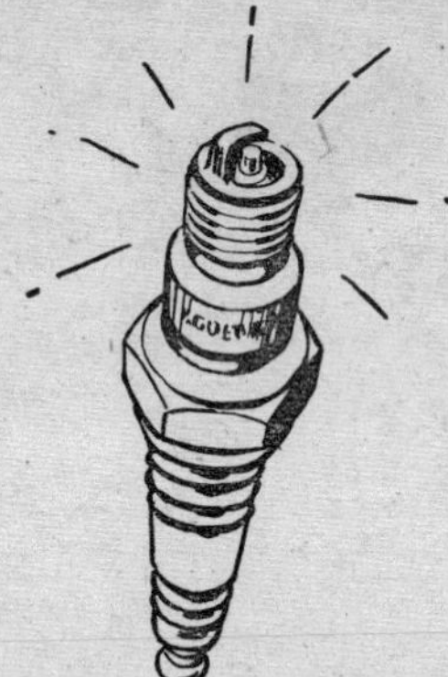

A GREY OR PALE-BROWN NOSE, DRY AND WITH LITTLE DEPOSIT, INDICATES PERFECT COMBUSTION.

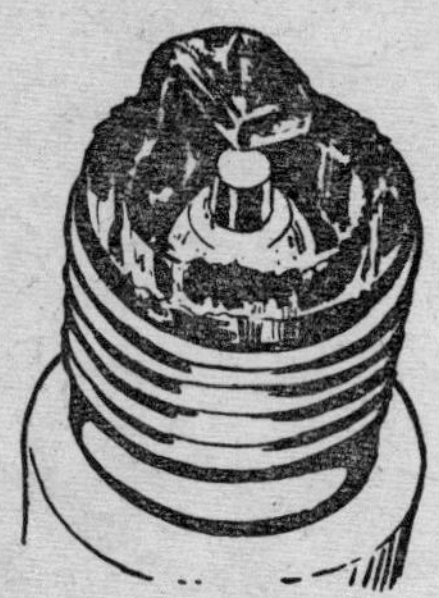

A BODY WITH GREASY BLACK DEPOSITS INDICATES EXCESSIVE OIL IN THE CYLINDER. PUT IN HOTTER PLUGS WHILE WAITING FOR REPAIRS.

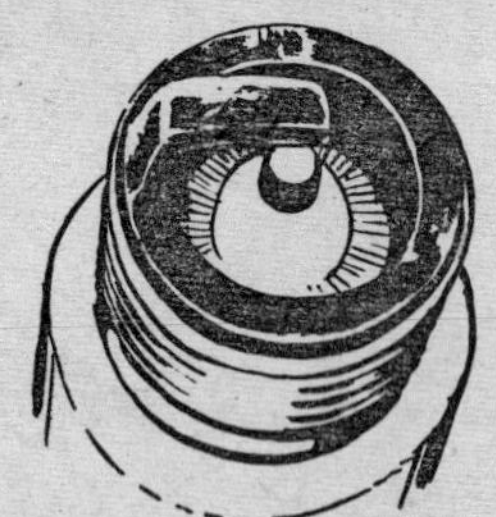

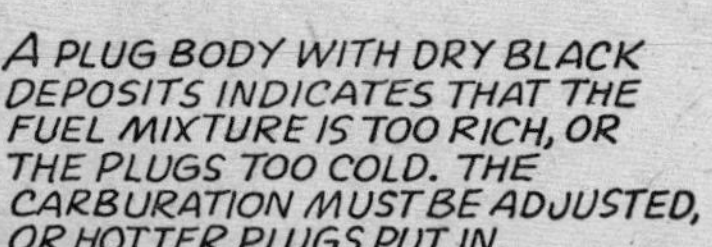

A PLUG BODY WITH DRY BLACK DEPOSITS INDICATES THAT THE FUEL MIXTURE IS TOO RICH, OR THE PLUGS TOO COLD. THE CARBURATION MUST BE ADJUSTED, OR HOTTER PLUGS PUT IN.

Smell of hot oil — check crankcase ventilation

FRED! COME AND HELP! THERE'S A SMELL OF BURNING OIL IN MY CAR, IT'S UNBEARABLE!
RIGHT, LET'S HAVE A LOOK.
THERE'S AN OIL LEAK ONTO THE EXHAUST PIPE, IT'S HAVING A GOOD FRY-UP. LET'S FIND THE LEAK AND CURE IT QUICKLY.
62

Hot and cold spark plugs

A PLUG WITH HEAVY CRUSTED DEPOSITS INDICATES POOR MAINTENANCE OF THE PLUGS OR THAT THE PLUGS ARE TOO COLD. YOU MUST CLEAN, ADJUST OR PUT IN HOTTER PLUGS.

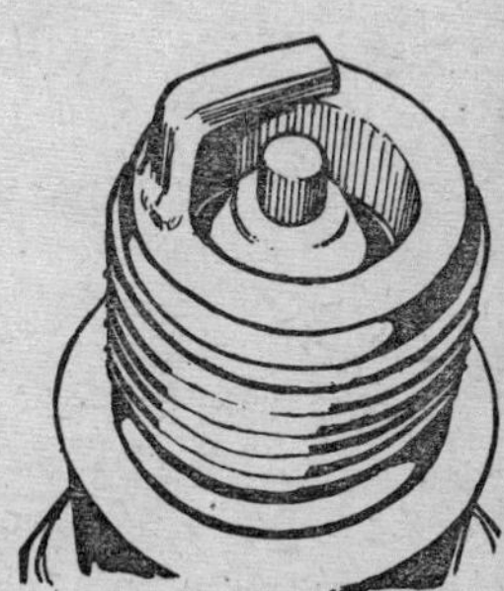

PLUG WITH MAT WHITE INSULATOR AND ELECTRODES TOO FAR APART IS TOO HOT AND HAS OVERHEATED. BUT THIS CAN ALSO COME FROM TOO WEAK A MIXTURE.

IN GENERAL, PLUGS WHICH ARE **TOO COLD** COULD CAUSE DIFFICULTIES IN STARTING, POOR IDLING, POOR PICK-UP AND HIGH FUEL CONSUMPTION.
PLUGS WHICH ARE **TOO HOT** CAUSE OVER-HEATING, A RISK OF PRE-IGNITION, FAILURES AT HIGH SPEEDS, AND CAN DAMAGE PISTONS.

Clutch slip

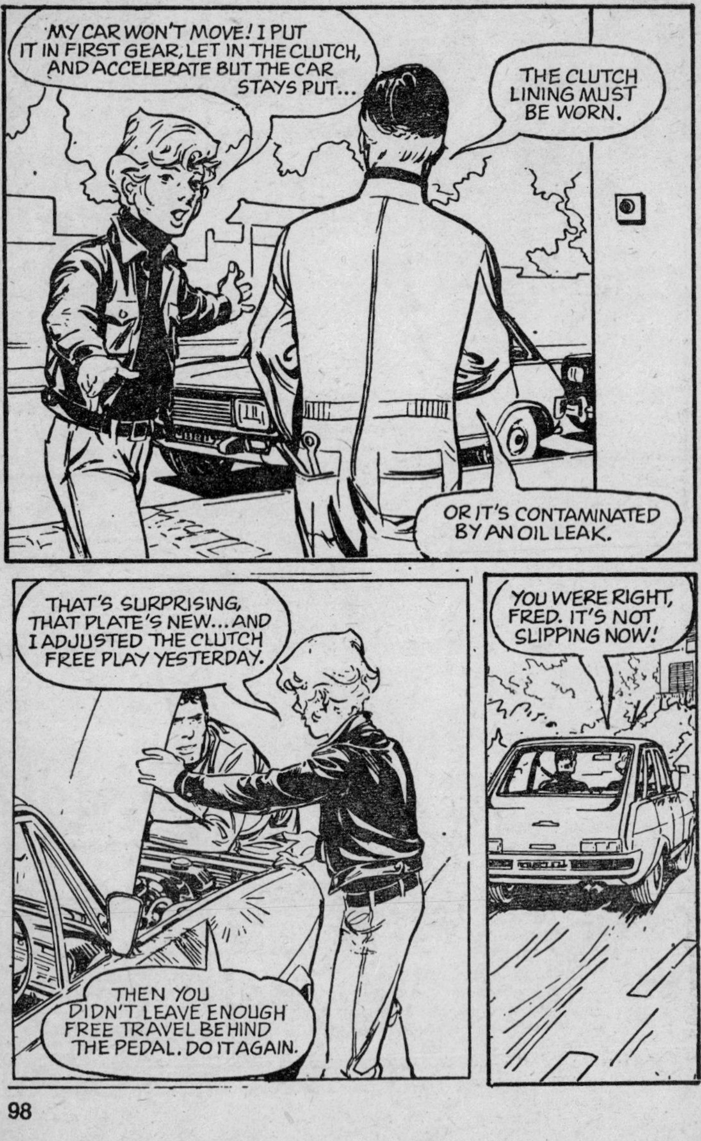

MY CAR WON'T MOVE! I PUT IT IN FIRST GEAR, LET IN THE CLUTCH, AND ACCELERATE BUT THE CAR STAYS PUT...

THE CLUTCH LINING MUST BE WORN.

OR IT'S CONTAMINATED BY AN OIL LEAK.

Clutch not disengaging

Poor gear changing

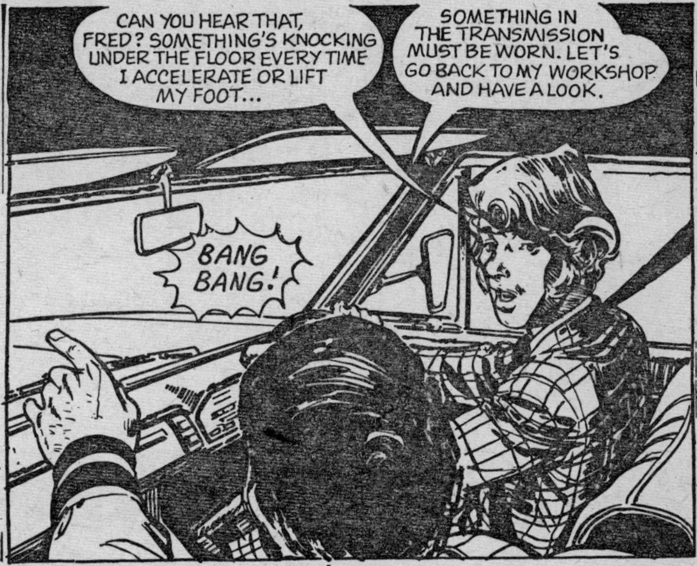

CAN YOU HEAR THAT, FRED? SOMETHING'S KNOCKING UNDER THE FLOOR EVERY TIME I ACCELERATE OR LIFT MY FOOT...

SOMETHING IN THE TRANSMISSION MUST BE WORN. LET'S GO BACK TO MY WORKSHOP AND HAVE A LOOK.

BANG BANG!

THERE'S A RATTLE UNDERNEATH EVERY TIME I ACCELERATE OR LIFT MY FOOT.
YOURS IS A FRONT WHEEL DRIVE CAR — MAYBE THE JOINTS ON THE DRIVE SHAFT ARE WORN OUT. LET ME TAKE THE WHEEL WILL YOU ?
NO DOUBT ABOUT IT, THE RATTLE GETS LOUDER WHEN YOU TURN THE WHEEL. THEY'RE GIVING UP.
THE JOINTS ARE PROTECTED BY THIS RUBBER BOOT, AND IT'S SPLIT. THE GREASE HAS ESCAPED AND THE JOINT HAS WORN, SO, IT MUST BE CHANGED.

Chapter 10

ADJUSTMENTS

From time to time parts of the car begin to wear, as they must in anything that moves. Often some means of adjustment is provided at the manufacturing stage, to take up the wear so that the mechanism can continue to function with the accuracy it had when new. It is simply a question of knowing which parts can be safely and successfuly adjusted and how.

Clutch play adjustment

Focusing the headlights

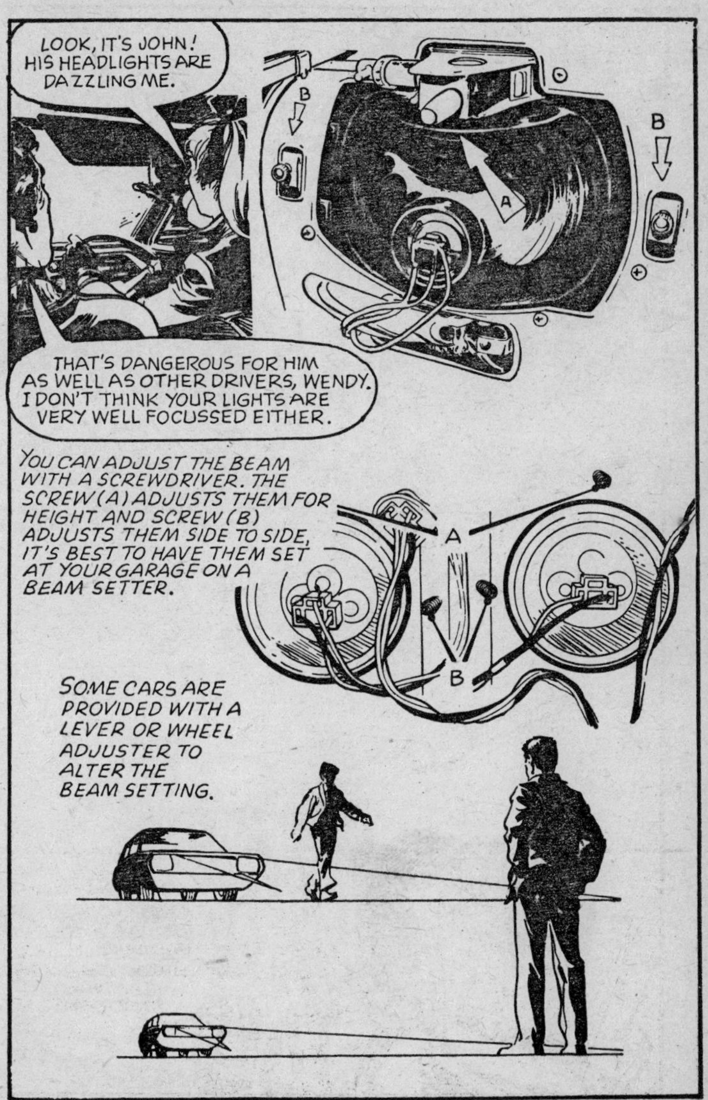

Cleaning the spark plugs

Checking the points

Checking the timing

Setting valve clearances

Setting valve clearances — the four stages

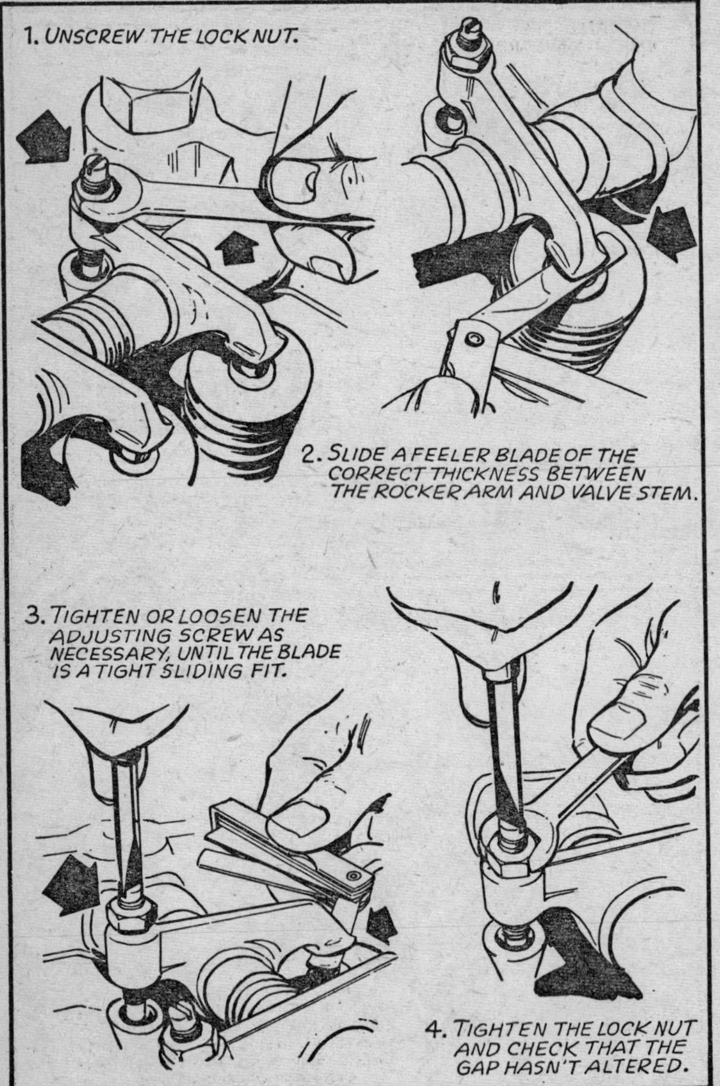

Fan belt adjustment

BUT I'D PUT THE HAND BRAKE ON...
BUT; WENDY, IT NEEDS ADJUSTING FROM TIME TO TIME TO TAKE UP WEAR.

THE HANDBRAKE SHOULD ENGAGE ON THE 3rd OR 4th CLICK. IF IT DOESN'T, LEAVE IT IN THIS POSITION AND SLIDE UNDER THE CAR.

YOU'LL FIND AN ADJUSTER WHICH STRETCHES TWO CABLES AT ONCE. UNSCREW THE LOCKNUT, TIGHTEN TO STRETCH THE CABLES, TIGHTEN THE LOCKNUT.
BUT ON SOME CARS, ADJUSTMENT CAN BE MADE ON THE HANDBRAKE LEVER, WITH A KNURLED WHEEL OR SPANNER (SEE HAND-BOOK).

Drum brake adjustment

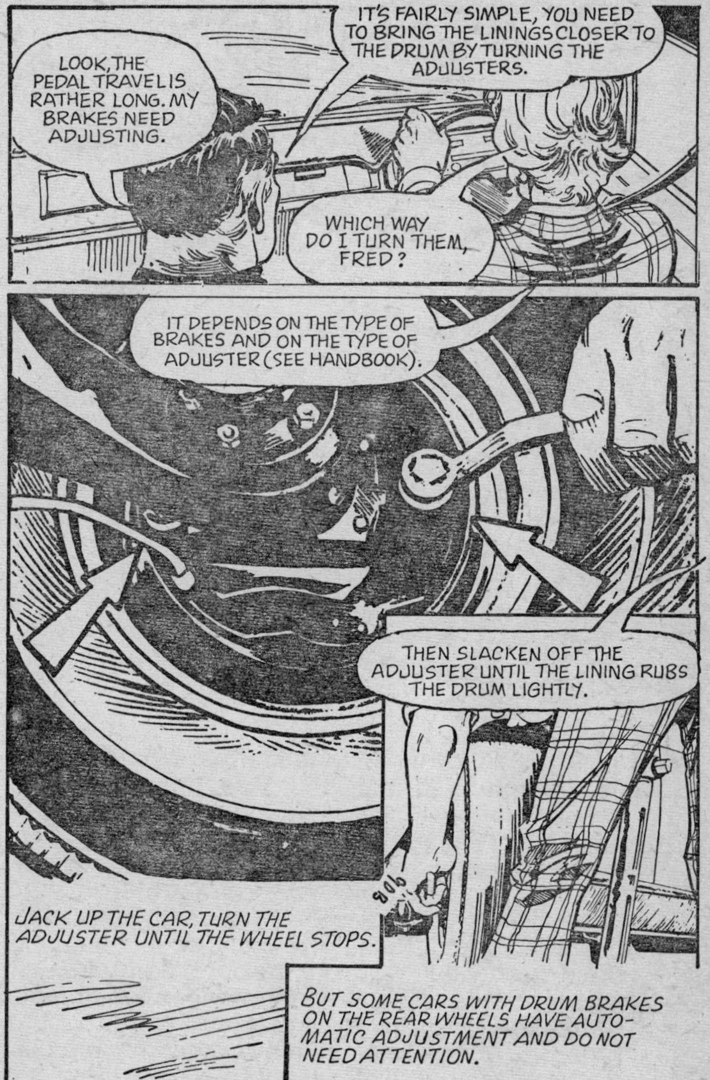

Chapter 11

REPLACEMENTS

Some parts cannot be adjusted, either because they are too complicated, like shock absorbers, or they are uneconomical to repair, such as the oil filter. These parts need replacement from time to time. When a replacement is needed make very sure that it is the correct part for your car. If in doubt go to the dealer armed with the engine and chassis number of your particular model. Design is constantly changing and the dealer will know from the car's numbers just when it was made and when any changes took place. Replacing parts with incorrect or non-standard equipment is uneconomical, may be bad for the car, or in some cases positively dangerous.

Changing a headlight bulb

Checking the air filter

Changing brake pads

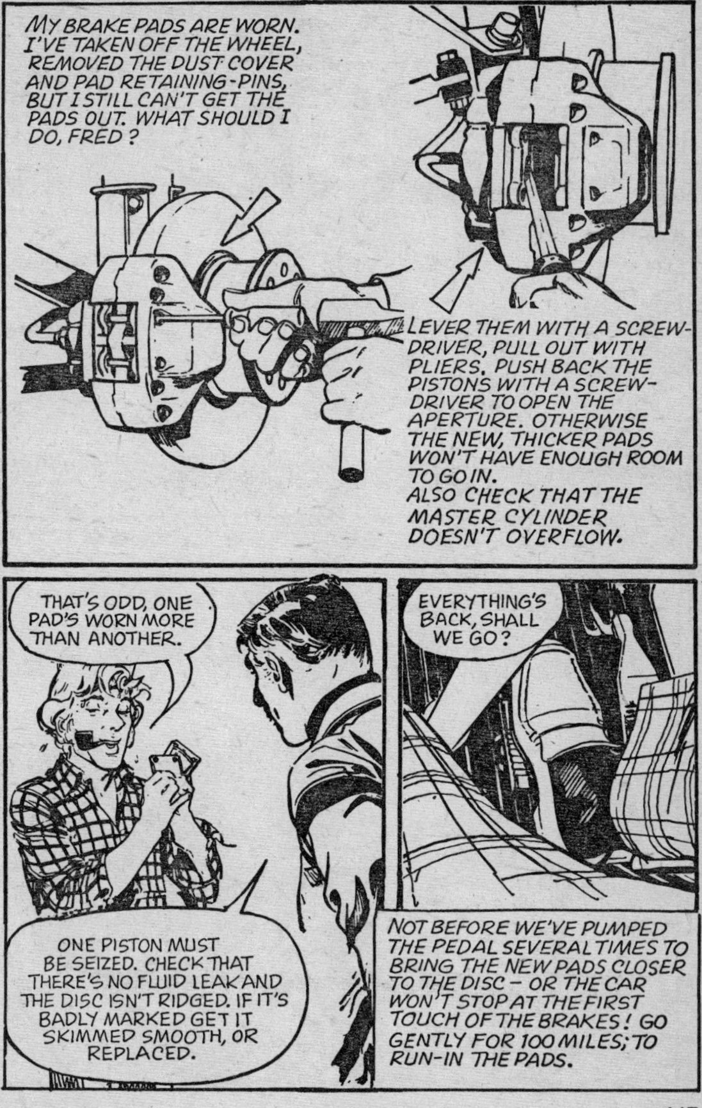

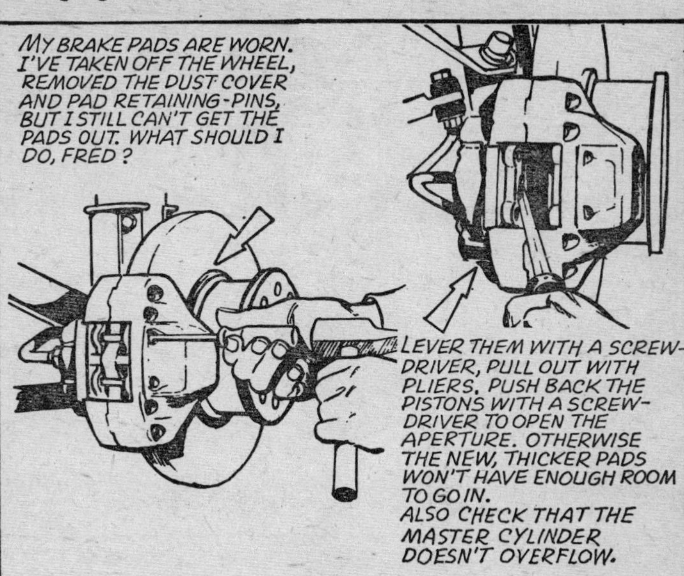

THAT'S ODD, ONE PAD'S WORN MORE THAN ANOTHER.

ONE PISTON MUST BE SEIZED. CHECK THAT THERE'S NO FLUID LEAK AND THE DISC ISN'T RIDGED. IF IT'S BADLY MARKED GET IT SKIMMED SMOOTH, OR REPLACED.

EVERYTHING'S BACK, SHALL WE GO?

NOT BEFORE WE'VE PUMPED THE PEDAL SEVERAL TIMES TO BRING THE NEW PADS CLOSER TO THE DISC – OR THE CAR WON'T STOP AT THE FIRST TOUCH OF THE BRAKES! GO GENTLY FOR 100 MILES; TO RUN-IN THE PADS.

Changing brake pads — floating caliper discs

GOOD, JOHN... BUT DON'T LET THE CALIPER HANG ON THE END OF THE BRAKE PIPE OR IT WILL BE DAMAGED. WHEN YOU HAVE PUT IT TOGETHER, PUMP THE BRAKE PEDAL SEVERAL TIMES MOVING OFF.

Bleeding the hydraulic system

Changing dampers

I'M GLAD YOU'RE HERE, FRED, I AM ABOUT TO CHANGE THE DAMPERS.

YES, BUT AFTER JACKING THE CAR UP, LOWER THE SUSPENSION ONTO AN AXLE STAND TO COMPRESS THE SPRING.

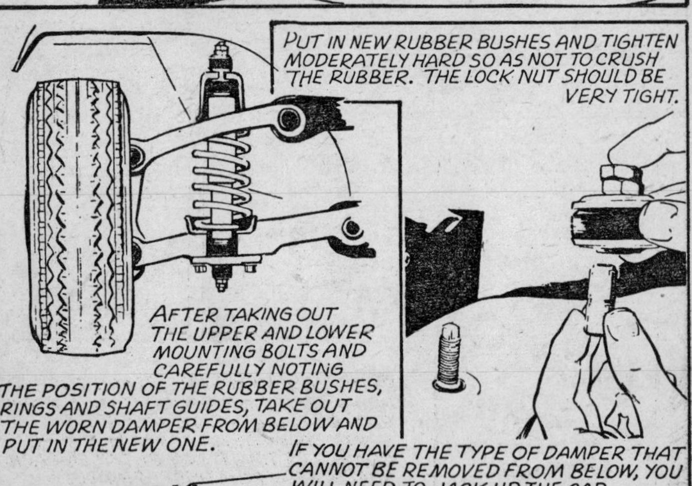

Retouching the paintwork

COMING TO THE PICTURES, JOHN?

NO, I'VE GOT TO REPAIR THIS WING.

IT'S ONLY A SUPERFICIAL SCRATCH, A GOOD POLISH WILL SOMETIMES DO THE TRICK...

...OR, IT CAN BE TAKEN OUT WITH A TOUCH-IN BRUSH.

NO, THE METAL'S DENTED— IT WILL TAKE SOME TIME... FIRST TO TAP IT OUT WITH A RUBBER-FACED HAMMER...

RUBBING DOWN THE METAL.

FILLING.

RUBBING DOWN THE FILLER.

PAINTING.

WITH THE SURFACE FILLED AND RUBBED DOWN, COVER ALL ROUND IT WITH NEWSPAPER SECURED BY ADHESIVE TAPE. SPRAY ON WITH AN AEROSOL, THREE COATS, LETTING IT DRY BETWEEN EACH, SHELTERED FROM DUST. FINALLY POLISH TO BLEND WITH THF EXISTING PAINT.

Chapter 12

ECONOMY DRIVING

Driving economically is nothing more than making the best use of the petrol that is being consumed. Petrol is burnt to provide heat that moves the car and any heat that is produced but not used to power the car is wasted. The heat loss in the radiator and in the hot gas of the exhaust is unavoidable with present designs of car engines, but there is still a lot of heat energy lost needlessly.

Careful adjustment

To begin, the engine must always be in top condition and all the adjustments made to this end. Wrong ignition timing, incorrect fuel/air mixtures in the carburettor, too low tyre pressures and an excess of friction, such as that produced by dragging brakes, will all result in higher petrol consumption.

Although there are many gadgets that claim to reduce fuel consumption, the best gadget of all is the driver's mind controlling the accelerator pedal. The engine fuel consumption is high at slow road speeds. It reduces as speed increases to a minimum of around two-thirds to three-quarters of the maximum speed of the car. It then increases again up to full throttle. Therefore in terms of economy it is a mistake to drive too slowly. It is equally a mistake to use a lower gear ratio than the engine needs to pull sweetly.

Speed and economy

The rate at which fuel is used is proportional to the rate of acceleration. So gentle acceleration and gentle changing up to a higher gear ratio as soon as possible can reduce the petrol flow needed for the engine. Once a reasonable speed has been reached it is better to maintain a constant throttle opening, than to keep accelerating up the hills and braking down the slopes to keep a steady speed. If you want to increase your speed it is most economical to let the car gather speed downhill.

Every time the brakes are applied, the moving energy of the car is changed into heat energy by brake friction. As the energy to move the car has been produced from the petrol burnt in the engine, the heat coming from the brakes must have originated in that petrol. So every time you brake you might just as well be pouring petrol on the road. By using your eyes to see what will happen further up the road, you can very often manage to be moving at the right speed when you get there, without using the brakes at all. For instance, if you look ahead and see a bend that you cannot round at your present speed, don't wait until you are nearly there and then brake hard. Lift your foot slightly from the accelerator and let the wind and tyre friction slow you down naturally. It is amazing just how far it is possible to travel using eyes and anticipation instead of brakes, and it is equally amazing how much fuel is saved and how smooth the ride becomes. Economy is not only saving petrol, but making the car, its tyres and brake linings last longer. Smooth driving with only essential braking does just this.

Dangerous coasting

Coasting in neutral with the engine switched off saves virtually nothing, but produces some very dangerous situations. There is no engine power to get you out of trouble, the vacuum servo ceases to work and makes brake pedal pressures much too high and, with modern cars, switched off ignition often means locked steering.

Dos and don'ts for economy

This list of hints will help you to see at a glance how you can alter your driving habits to make your car and your petrol last longer.

DO

Drive off straight away, but gently. Close the choke as soon as possible. Accelerate smoothly. Anticipate what is going to happen. Use the highest gear possible without strain. Keep the tyres at the right pressure. Make sure the brakes are not binding. Remove a roof rack when it is not wanted. Keep to a steady speed. Switch off electrical gadgets you don't need.

DON'T

Warm up the engine for long periods. Forget to close the choke. Play first away from traffic lights. Keep changing gear unnecessarily. Slip the clutch to keep the engine speed up. Brake hard from high speeds except in an emergency. Coast in neutral. Open the windows at high speed. Fill the petrol tank to the brim, so it can spill. Carry more of a load in the car than you need.

Using too much fuel — check everything

THAT WAS A GOOD TRIP.
THE TYRES LOOK SOFT... OH WELL, IT'S NOT SERIOUS.
YES, IT IS, JOHN! IT INCREASES FUEL CONSUMPTION. PUT UP PRESSURES BY 2 OR 3 LBS. BUT KEEP THE DIFFERENTIAL BETWEEN FRONT AND REAR.
TYRE PRESSURES SHOULD NEVER FALL BELOW MANUFACTURERS' RECOMMENDATIONS.
WE'LL HAVE GOOD FIRES THIS WINTER!
THIS TYRE ISN'T WEARING NORMALLY. THE WHEELS MUST BE OUT OF TRACK. THAT CAUSES EXCESSIVE FUEL CONSUMPTION, TOO.
YES, BUT DON'T LET'S LOAD UP ANY MORE. 150 lbs OVERLOAD EQUALS AN EXTRA TWO m.p.g.
I'LL HAVE TO FILL UP. I THINK I'LL GET TWO-STAR – IT'S CHEAPER.
NO YOU DON'T. IT'S FALSE ECONOMY UNLESS YOU HAVE A LOW COMPRESSION ENGINE. USE THE RIGHT GRADE.

MY CAR USES TOO MUCH FUEL IN TOWN.
BECAUSE YOU DRIVE ROUGHLY, WENDY. DON'T PANIC AT THE LAST MINUTE, BE PREPARED. LET THE CAR FLOW IN THE TRAFFIC STREAM.
AND YOU'RE SURPRISED AT USING TOO MUCH FUEL? IF YOU ACCELERATE HARD, YOU WASTE ENERGY SLOWING DOWN. DRIVE FLEXIBLY.
SHE'S NERVOUS, ISN'T SHE?
PUT BACK THE CHOKE AS SOON AS THE ENGINE'S WARMED UP. WE'VE BEEN DRIVING MORE THAN THREE MINUTES SO IT'S REACHED ITS TEMPERATURE NOW.

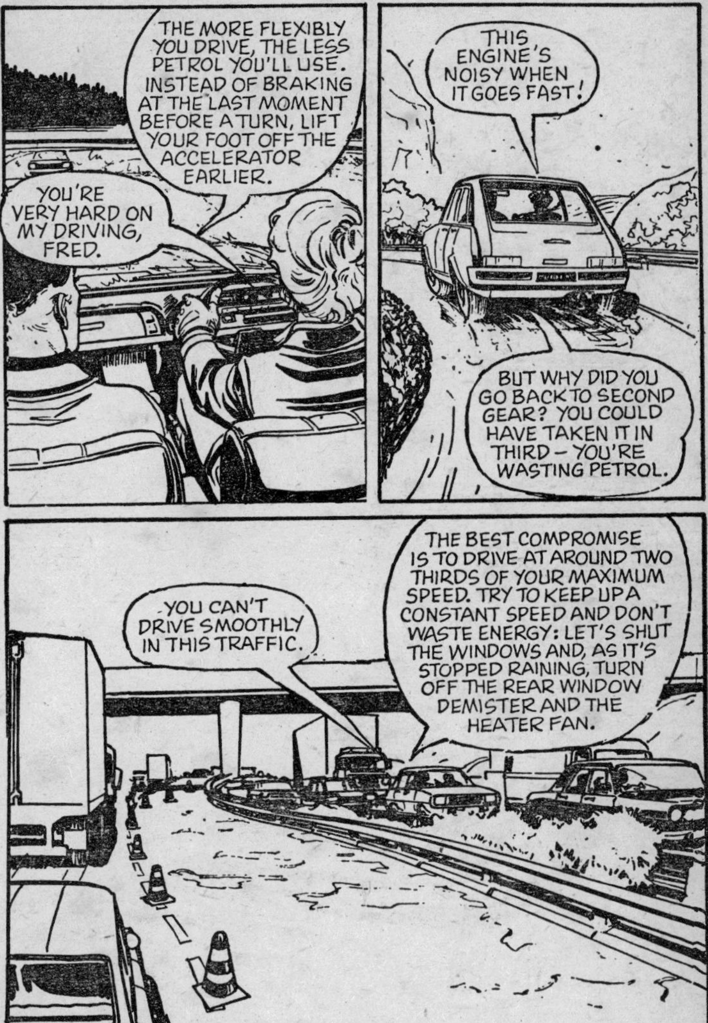

YOU CAN'T DRIVE SMOOTHLY IN THIS TRAFFIC.

THE BEST COMPROMISE IS TO DRIVE AT AROUND TWO THIRDS OF YOUR MAXIMUM SPEED. TRY TO KEEP UP A CONSTANT SPEED AND DON'T WASTE ENERGY: LET'S SHUT THE WINDOWS AND, AS IT'S STOPPED RAINING, TURN OFF THE REAR WINDOW DEMISTER AND THE HEATER FAN.